Michele Elliott is a teacher, psychologist and mother of two boys. She has worked with children and families since 1968, and is on the Advisory Councils of ChildLine and the NSPCC. She has chaired World Health Organisation and Home Office working groups, and has been awarded a Winston Churchill Fellowship. She is the author of fourteen other books, including *501 Ways to be a Good Parent, Keeping Safe: A Practical Guide to Talking with Children, Feeling Happy, Feeling Safe*, a colour picture book for young children, and the series *The Willow Street Kids*, for primary aged children. She is often on the television and radio discussing issues about children and writes a regular column for *Family Circle* magazine. In 1984 Michele founded the children's charity KIDSCAPE, which works to keep children safe from bullying, abuse and other dangers.

D1589033

Also by Michele Elliott
and available from Hodder & Stoughton

501 Ways to be a Good Parent
Keeping Safe: A Practical Guide
to Talking with Children
Feeling Happy, Feeling Safe

101 Ways to Deal with Bullying

A Guide for Parents

Michele Elliott

Hodder & Stoughton

Copyright © 1997 by Michele Elliott

The right of Michele Elliott to be identified as the Author of
the Work has been asserted by her in accordance with the
Copyright, Designs and Patents Act 1988.

First published in Great Britain in 1997 by Hodder & Stoughton
A division of Hodder Headline PLC

10 9 8 7 6 5 4 3 2 1

A CIP catalogue record for this title
is available from the British Library

ISBN 0 340 69519 6

Typeset by Hewer Text Composition Services, Edinburgh
Printed and bound in Great Britain by
Clays Ltd, St Ives plc

Hodder and Stoughton
A Division of Hodder Headline PLC
338 Euston Road
London NW1 3BH

For Donald Brooksbank
who loved children

CONTENTS

1

WHAT IS BULLYING?

Thirteen-year-old Katherine was stripped to the waist on the school playground by a gang of twelve boys and girls. She was photographed, forced onto her knees and made to beg to get her clothes back. She told no one what had happened. Instead she tried to kill herself. That's how her mother found out about the bullying which had gone on long before this last incident.

When Katherine's mother contacted the school to complain, she was told by the headteacher that 'this was just a bit of fun that got out of hand'. The headteacher then went on to say more about his philosophy which I will relate shortly.

James, aged seven, was bullied by three nine-year-olds every day on the way to school. They started out by taunting him and then went on to kick and punch him and take his lunch which they threw away. James's mother discovered the bullying when she questioned why he was always so hungry when he came home.

Eleven-year-old Sonia was sent to Coventry by the girls in her class. They refused to sit with her, would not talk to her, whispered whenever she was around and made her life miserable. Sonia told her father about the bullying and he went to the school. The teacher was appalled by what she heard and sorted it out immediately.

This teacher was certainly more enlightened than Katherine's headteacher. Katherine's mother was told by him that: 'Bullying is no big deal. In fact, it is probably good that children experience it. We just have to accept that bullying is part of human nature, something children must learn to cope with if they are to be prepared for the future and the rough and tumble of life.'

What dribble! Fortunately Katherine's headteacher is in the minority. (In fact Katherine is no longer in that school and she is doing well.) Most teachers now accept that bullying is wrong and should be stopped. Why on earth should we raise children who think that the best way to get along in life is to be a bully? Why should we raise children who lose their confidence and sense of self-worth because some other children need a victim to pick on? Bullying is not a natural part of growing up. Nor does it prepare children for the future. As for human nature, I certainly know hundreds of people who do not bully others, so if it is part of human nature I guess they aren't human!

If your child is being bullied or has been singled out as a bully, the last thing you want to hear is that you should just ignore the problem and consider it a normal part of growing up. You shouldn't and it isn't. To help you determine what is happening to your child, it may be useful to look at the definitions and signs and symptoms of bullying.

DEFINING BULLYING

Bullying is the use of aggression with the intention of hurting another person. It results in pain and distress to the victim, who has in no way provoked the bullying. Usually the bullying is a campaign over time against a child, but sometimes there can be just one incident.

Dan Olweus, the world-renowned expert in the field of bullying, defines bullying as a child being 'exposed, repeatedly and over time, to negative actions on the part of one or more students'. He also says there must be an 'imbalance of strength'.[1] So that two children of equal physical or psychological strength quarrelling or fighting may not be a case of bullying. Usually the victim of bullying is helpless against what is happening and those bullying are deliberately trying to harm the victim in some way.

Bullying can be:

Physical	pushing, kicking, punching, hitting, or any use of or threatened use of physical violence
Verbal	name-calling, sarcasm, spreading rumours, nasty teasing, writing awful things about someone, leaving hurtful notes
Emotional	excluding, being deliberately unfriendly, tormenting, racial taunts, threatening or rude gestures
Menacing	demanding money or possessions or to copy homework, demanding the victim's or bystander's silence when bullying has taken place

SIGNS AND SYMPTOMS

Seven-year-old Rosemary was finding every excuse in the world not to go to school. At first her parents thought nothing of it, thinking that she was suffering from a tummy bug. After several days at home, her mother insisted that she go back to school. The night before she was to go back, Rosemary had bad dreams and wet the bed. The next morning she asked her mother to drive her to school. Within an hour of Rosemary arriving at school, the secretary rang to say that Rosemary was still feeling unwell and could her mother please collect her. It took three weeks before the real cause of her symptoms of illness came out. Another child had taken a dislike to Rosemary and was bullying her at every turn, including harassment on the way to and from school. Hence Rosemary's request to be driven the short distance to her primary school.

All parents need to be aware of the signs that a child might be being bullied because, like Rosemary, your child may not come right out and say what is happening. If your child shows some of the following behaviours or signs, ask him or her about bullying.

Children may:

- be frightened of walking to or from school or change their normal route to school

- not want to go on the school bus

- beg you to drive them to school

- be unwilling to go to school or feel ill every morning

- begin truanting

- begin doing poorly in their school work

- come home with clothes or books destroyed

What is Bullying?

- become surly towards family members

- come home starving (bully has taken dinner money)

- become withdrawn, start stammering, lack confidence

- become distressed and anxious, stop eating

- attempt or threaten suicide

- cry themselves to sleep, have nightmares

- ask for money or begin stealing (to pay the bully)

- refuse to say what's wrong (frightened of the bully)

- have unexplained scratches, bruises, etc.

- begin to bully other children or siblings

- become aggressive and unreasonable

Obviously these behaviours and symptoms could indicate problems other than bullying. For example, a surly, withdrawn child may be on the verge of becoming a 'hormonally driven' teenager. However, if your child exhibits several of these signs or behaviours, then you should suspect bullying.

ASK DIRECTLY

If your child does show some of these signs, then ask him or her if bullying is a problem. Be direct. Say, 'I think you are being bullied or threatened and I'm worried about you. Let's talk about it.' If your child doesn't tell you immediately, say that you are there and willing to listen, night or day, when he or she is ready to talk. Then keep a watchful eye – kids can become quite desperate when they are being bullied and do dumb things like run away or take an overdose because it all seems so hopeless to them.

WHERE AND WHEN

Most bullying takes place in and around the school or on the way to and from school. Children and young people report to KIDSCAPE, the children's charity which deals with bullying and child-abuse prevention, that the majority of bullying at school happens:

- in the toilets
- in the lunch room
- on the playground or school playing-fields
- while passing to classes
- on the way to and from school

Although some children report being bullied in the classroom, it is much more usual for the bullying to take place out of sight of the school staff. This can lead to some staff

What is Bullying?

members genuinely feeling that 'no bullying goes on in this school'. The best way for schools to find out where and when bullying is occurring is to give the students an anonymous questionnaire asking very specific questions. Then supervision and monitoring can eliminate much of the bullying.

WHO BULLIES?

Before discussing some of the things you can do if your child is being bullied (chapter 2), or if your child is being a bully (chapter 3), let's briefly look at who the bullies are. The stereotype of the big, mean, nasty boy is one that usually comes to mind when the word bully is mentioned. The reality is that bullies can be any shape or size and that girls are equally as capable as boys of bullying. Some studies indicate that boys are more likely to bully using physical violence, while girls are more likely to use verbal harassment. There is some limited evidence from helplines (see below, Is Bullying Worse Today?) that these patterns may be changing.

As a brief guide, the children and young people who frequently bully do seem to share some common characteristics. They often:

- feel inadequate to cope with everyday events
- are bullied themselves within their families
- come from families which extol the 'virtues' of bullying
- are victims of some kind of abuse
- don't know how or are not allowed to show feelings
- are not succeeding in school
- feel no sense of self-worth

There are also bullies who are self-confident spoilt children who have always had their own way, expect it as their right and are prepared to bully to get it.

Some bullies just enjoy being 'in charge' and may get status from their position as 'leader'. These children are confident but often obnoxious to anyone they don't consider to be their equal.

Then we have the children who may bully others once in a while because they have some sort of upheaval in their lives, such as the birth of a baby, the death of someone they love, rejection from a friend, being the victim themselves of bullying, a run-in with a family member or a teacher, boredom or a whole host of other problems which might lead them to lashing out at another child. (See chapter 3 for more information about helping bullies.)

WHY BULLY?

Bullying is intended to humiliate the victim and most bullies know exactly what they are doing. Bullying makes them feel powerful and in control. There are times, however, when the bully doesn't realise how much harm she or he is causing. Perhaps they go along with the crowd and say hurtful things without thinking through what they are doing. Perhaps they bully because they are secretly frightened that if they don't, they will be the next victim. Perhaps they bully because they are bored. Whatever the reason, it is no comfort to the victim, whose life has been made miserable.

WHO ARE THE VICTIMS?

In my experience, most victims of bullying are sensitive, intelligent, gentle children who have good relationships with their parents. They don't come from families full of conflict and shouting, so when bullies attack them, they do not know what to do. They frequently ask why someone would want to bully them – they've done nothing to deserve it and they haven't been treated this way before. The sad fact is that, from the bully's viewpoint, they make excellent targets because they are nice and won't fight back. They might even cry, a bonus for the bully. If you could point out one 'fault' of these victims, it would be that they are too nice! In a school which doesn't tolerate bullying, they have no problems.

There are, however, some children who seem to get bullied everywhere – at school, parties, activities, clubs, you name it and they are bullied. These are the children who seem to invite bullying and almost thrive on the negative attention they get when they are bullied. It is as if the bullying confirms their opinions of themselves that they are worthless and deserve what is happening to them. There may be problems in the lives of these children which are very similar to the problems of the bullies mentioned above. Or they may have been bullied right from the day when they started school and never recovered their confidence. Whatever the reason, they seem to go through life as perpetual victims. (See chapter 2 for suggestions on helping victims.)

HOW WIDESPREAD IS BULLYING?

Whenever someone says that 'We don't have a problem because there are no bullies in our school', I am suspicious. Either they have actually set up a no bullying ethos without defining it, or work in a school with two students who are best friends, or they just don't want to know. One mother rang KIDSCAPE to say that her sixteen-year-old son had been bullied so badly that he tried to commit suicide. The response from that headteacher was that the boy should 'pull himself together because life was tough all over'. On the other hand, there are very enlightened headteachers and others doing their best to ensure that children and young people are free from the torment of bullying.

Recent studies have shown that bullying takes place in every type of school and occurs in all classes and cultures. It is much more widespread than was previously recognised. Bullying also occurs in institutions, the work place, religious organisations and agencies of every kind. It seems that little bullies grow up to be big bullies and turn to adult victims after they leave school. Of course, many of these bullies also make life impossible for their own children and families.

The first nationwide survey of bullying was carried out by KIDSCAPE between 1984 and 1986. Four thousand children aged five to sixteen were interviewed from a random selection of fourteen schools from South-East London, Surrey, Newcastle, East Sussex, the Midlands and Devon. The children were asked about their main worries and concerns. Although they talked about everything from getting lost to being frightened by bad dreams, the majority (68%)

complained of being bullied at some time. Most of the incidents occurred when travelling to or from school or in school. The bullying usually took place when no adult was present.

The children were then asked in more detail about their experiences: 38% of them had been bullied more than once or had experienced a particularly terrifying bullying incident. Approximately 10% of the children and young people seemed to be chronically and severely bullied to the point where it was affecting their everyday lives. Some of these children were terrified of going to school, often played truant, were ill, or had attempted suicide. It is this severely bullied group which is the most worrying as their behaviour is self-destructive. Eighty per cent of the reported bullies were boys, 20% girls. The vast majority of the bullies were at least one year older than their victims; many were two or more years older.[2] In more recent surveys carried out by KIDSCAPE, the number of girls reported as bullies has increased. This is most likely because children and young people are beginning to realise that bullying includes being called names and other forms of verbal and emotional torment, as well as being physically attacked.

Other studies have been carried out in schools since KIDSCAPE's pioneering survey. Some recent research was organised by the Department for Education-funded Sheffield Bullying Project. It found that 27% of pupils in junior/middle schools in Sheffield were bullied at least once during termtime, and 10% said that they were bullied once a week. Figures for secondary schools were lower, although still far from negligible: 10% bullied at least once during termtime and 4% bullied once a week.[3]

It is probably reasonable to conclude that at any one time about one in seven children are involved in bullying either as victims or bullies. However, over a whole school career even more children will have been affected by bullying.[4]

IS BULLYING WORSE TODAY?

Some adults say that bullying went on in their youth, but that it was not nearly as bad as it is today. That is disputed by some victims, who say that it was just as terrible, but no one talked about it. It is difficult to say because we have no statistics from the 'olden days'. From our experience at KIDSCAPE, I would have to say that bullying *is* on the increase and that it is getting more nasty and violent. I base this on the calls that we have had to our helpline and the letters we have received over the past several years.

We have had a dramatic increase of calls from parents whose children are being viciously physically attacked by girls. Previously the calls about girls bullying tended to include calling names and being cruel in a verbal or emotional way. Now many parents tell about incidents where their daughters have had their noses and arms broken, been given black eyes, had their clothes torn off and been subjected to sexual assaults by *girl* bullies. We have had only a few calls about boys being bullied by girls in this way, though we have had some calls about girls making crude comments or sexual gestures to boys. This may have been a hidden problem in the past, but I suspect girls have become more aggressive and it is showing up in the way they bully.

Another worrying trend is the increase in violence by very young children (see chapter 7) and the use of weapons by bullies of all ages. I think that the amount of gratuitous graphic violence witnessed by children in films and on some television programmes does affect their behaviour. Common sense tells me that children learn from what they see and experience. I know my children do. However, many experts would disagree with me so I leave you to make your own judgements.

IT IS ONLY TEASING

What is the difference between teasing and bullying? The dictionary defines teasing as 'to annoy or harass by persistent mocking or poking fun, or playful fooling'. The first part of this definition fits my idea of bullying – annoying and harassing people and making fun of them. But I have no problem with what I consider teasing – the second part of the dictionary definition. When I was a child, there was a lot of teasing in our household. It was always in good humour and we all enjoyed it and joined in. Whenever the teasing got out of hand, it was instantly stopped by my grandmother. It was definitely not bullying and it did instil in me a lasting sense of humour which has stood me in good stead over the years.

Teaching children the 'proper' way to tease and to be teased may help them to develop the confidence to deal with some bullying. The ground rules for teasing are simple:

- teasing is only allowed when both parties are having fun

- teasing is stopped as soon as one party wishes

An example of affectionate teasing which my sister and I still do to each other is about age. I was one year and three weeks older than my sister. So for three glorious weeks I was two years older than she was. I would be eight while she still had to wait three weeks to be seven. Oh yes, I teased her about it. But my father told her to wait until I turned thirty and she was still only twenty-eight. Well, that sister of mine did just that. On my thirtieth birthday she rang me to 'gloat' that she was still a 'young twenty-eight'. Imagine waiting all those years to tease me back. Serves me right, I reckon.

CORRECTIVE COMMENTS

Keep in mind that sometimes children make what I call 'corrective comments'. Although these comments might be hurtful and should perhaps not be made by other children or young people, they are an age-old way of letting people know they are out of line or that they need to stop doing something. An example of this was a child I worked with whom I will call Henry. Henry was a great character, but he had one obnoxious habit. He would not blow his nose and awful bits were always hanging off his nose. When these bits overwhelmed him he would wipe everything on his sleeves. You can imagine how pleasant it was to sit next to him at lunch. His parents talked to him, gave him tissues and did their best to get him to stop, but he could not be bothered to get out a tissue. The teachers also tried with no success to get Henry to be civilised.

Henry did change, but only after the other kids made comments and told him plainly what they thought. You might call it bullying; I call it peer pressure and sometimes it is the only way kids learn. Henry is still a great character, but his nose is clean and he is a popular boy.

MYTHS ABOUT BULLYING

'I was bullied at school and it didn't do me any harm'

This is often said quite aggressively as if the person is trying to convince him or herself that they are unaffected. The person may still be ashamed of the fact that they were unable to deal with the bullying themselves. They may never have faced up to what was done to them and how it affected them.

'Bullying is just a normal part of growing up'

It doesn't have to be. To say to children or teenagers that they should suffer bullying and that it is OK and normal is totally unacceptable. Some victims remain victims for a long time or even become bullies and perpetuate the problem. If we feed the myth, telling them, overtly or by messages of acceptance, that bullying is normal then we fail children.

It is possible to create an environment in which bullying is not tolerated and in which aggression and violence are viewed as negative and wholly inappropriate types of behaviour.

What is Bullying?

'It's character-building'

Why does a child have to be tormented to the edge of despair in order to have their character 'built'? Character-destructive might be a more apt description. You can 'build' a child's character far more successfully by using positive role-models and by encouraging responsible, kind and helpful behaviour.

'It'll make a man (woman) of him (her)'

This translates as 'You only become a man when you have suffered all sorts of beatings/thefts/tauntings in silence.' Why should a child be forced to suffer agonies in silence in order to become some sort of hero?

'There was bullying when I was at school but it didn't hurt anyone'

A comment usually made by a very hectoring and aggressive politician who had never recognised that he himself was a tremendous bully. He was oblivious to any suffering he might have caused people along the way.

'Sticks and stones can break your bones but names can never hurt you'

Anyone who believes this has never seen children reduced to despair by taunts like 'fatty', 'four-eyes', 'taphead', 'slag', 'spaz', 'Honky', 'Paki'. Names can hurt worse than sticks and stones and the hurt can last longer.

'Don't tell or you're a grass'

This myth is one of the most destructive. Bullying thrives in a climate of secrecy and fear. Unfortunately, for some children, telling *has* made the bullying worse. That is because the situation has been badly handled and the bully learns that not only are there no consequences to his or her actions, but that bullying is more or less condoned.

Victims must be encouraged to tell and to see that telling works. Children and young people are frightened that telling will make it worse. But not telling strengthens the bully's hand and makes him or her feel that they can continue bullying. Telling makes the problem public. The bully's greatest shield is anonymity.

WHAT HARM CAN IT DO?

KIDSCAPE gets hundreds of letters and telephone calls weekly about bullying. We have scores of letters, in which children tell of fear, threats, violence, bribery (money or sweets being extorted by bullies), ostracism and sexual and racial attacks. Each letter represents a small personal tragedy.

Imagine the terror of sitting in class, wondering what the bullies are going to do to you when you go to the toilet or try to eat your lunch.

Linda, now a mother of three, remembers what it was like:

I woke up every morning for three years hoping it was the weekend or a school holiday. If it was, I was happy.

What is Bullying?

If it wasn't, I closed my eyes again and prayed that my mother would let me stay home. I knew when I got to school that my life would be hell, but I never told my parents why I tried to stay home so often. I faked every illness under the sun, but sometimes I didn't have to pretend. The stress and tension were so bad that I did have severe headaches and stomach upsets. The main cause of my acute distress was a girl called Charlotte.

Charlotte was mean, vicious and vindictive. She enjoyed seeing me in pain. The bullying was verbal at first. For some reason I will never know, she started calling me names like ugly, fat, smelly. I might have been too sensitive, but I reacted by trying to please her and apologising for – heaven knows what, just being alive, I guess. I asked her why she hated me and what had I ever done to her. That was like waving a red flag to a bull. She saw it as a sign of weakness and homed in for the kill.

Over the next three years, she and her little gang of girls made me cry every day over something. I actually ended up feeling ugly, fat and smelly, though I was none of those things. When they got tired of calling me names, they pushed and shoved me in the halls, took my lunch away and threw it in the rubbish, stole my books and homework so I got into trouble with the teachers, followed me home and tripped me up and once ripped my jumper.

The odd thing is that I could not tell what was happening. I was so ashamed and thought that perhaps the bullying was my fault. It took me a long time to really trust anyone. I thought that anyone who tried to be friends with me would soon find out that I wasn't worth knowing so I kept myself to myself.

The bullying stopped when I left that school, but the effects linger on. If something goes wrong I automatically blame myself. I worry that my children will be bullied and watch for every little sign that something is amiss.

I wish now that I had told my parents. I know they would have helped me, but no one talked about bullying back then. Thank goodness there are organisations now dealing with it. I wouldn't wish bullying on my worst enemy – not even on Charlotte.

Bullying can have alarming long-term effects on both the victims and bullies. Victims tend to lack self-esteem, have difficulty trusting people, feel depressed and sometimes find themselves being bullied in later life at work or in relationships. Some adults say that they had difficulty in school because they were so worried about bullying – so their education has suffered as a result. According to a long-term study by Dan Olweus, boys who bully are four times more likely to end up in prison than the general population and to be involved in repeated antisocial behaviour as young adults. Another study has shown that fathers who were bullies at school are more likely to have sons who also bully others.

I have talked with parents whose children have run away, played truant, turned to drugs and solvents, become withdrawn, angry or aggressive, failed in school and even committed suicide because of bullying. It is a heart-wrenching experience to try to help them cope with the unnecessary and senseless death of their child, when you know that, had someone taken effective action, their child would still be alive. The parents blame themselves, which is understandable. But most bullying is school based and, *if* the school knew about the bullying but did nothing to stop it, then I'm afraid I have to lay the blame with the school. There are many things schools can do. (See chapter 6, Working with the School.)

BYSTANDERS

One other group of children who are harmed by bullying are rarely thought about – they are the bystanders. When an incident of bullying occurs, there are often children or young people who stand by and watch or see what is happening and walk on. These children are affected by the bullying in several ways:

- they feel guilty about not intervening or getting help
- they feel anxious that they might be the next victims
- they feel powerless and upset

On a recent television programme, I was sitting next to a man who turned to me to confess his twenty-year-old guilt at not having helped a classmate who was being bullied. 'I think I was just as responsible for the bullying as the bully,' he said. I agree with his sentiments.

IT HARMS US ALL

So bullying harms us all – the victims, the bullies and the bystanders. We need to teach all our children that bullying is wrong and that everyone has a duty to stop it, or get help if they can't.

POINTS TO REMEMBER

There are some basic facts about bullying that are, in my opinion, indisputable:

1. No one deserves to be bullied.

2. Most children and young people who are victims of bullying need adult help to stop the bullying.

3. We should never ignore serious bullying.

4. Bullies who get away with bullying learn that it is a good way to get what they want. Their behaviour carries on into their adult lives.

5. Children who stand by and watch someone being bullied are affected by what they see and by the fact that they didn't help in some way.

6. Children who are chronic victims of bullying become depressed, have low self-esteem, lack confidence, become withdrawn and often full of rage.

7. Schools have a responsibility to protect children and young people from bullying.

8. Bullying is always cruel, whether it is name-calling, exclusion from the group, hitting or making someone do something they don't want to do.

9. Bullying always involves an imbalance of power between the bully and the victim.

10. Bullying can be stopped when there is a commitment from the adults.

1 Olweus, D. *Bullying at School, What we know and what we can do*, Blackwell, 1995.

2 Elliott, M. *The KIDSCAPE Primary Child Protection Programme*, KIDSCAPE, 1994.

3. Whitney, I. & Smith, P. K. 'A survey of the nature & extent of bullying in junior/middle & secondary schools' in *Press Educational Research*, Vol. 35, No. 1, Spring 1993.

4 Pearce, J. in *Bullying: A Practical Guide to Coping for Schools*, ed. M. Elliott, 1997.

2

HOW TO HELP VICTIMS

Fourteen-year-old Michael had always been popular and successful in school. In the space of a few weeks all that changed out of recognition. He became withdrawn, grumpy and reluctant to wake up in the mornings to get to school on time. His parents thought he had reached those teenage years when hormones seem to blast the most even-tempered young people into a snarling orbit around the rest of the world. They decided to just give Michael a wide berth and hope he would snap out of it. The situation got worse when the deputy headteacher rang to say that Michael had been truanting.

Michael's parents sat down with him and tried to find out what was happening. Michael said that nothing was the matter, he was just tired of school and didn't want to go. His parents took him to the doctor, but no one seemed to be able to figure out what was bothering Michael. His parents made an appointment to take their son to a counsellor. Two days before they were due to see the counsellor, Michael broke down and told his father that all his friends had turned on him and he had become the victim of sustained bullying.

After much talking and tears, it emerged that Michael felt ashamed of being bullied and didn't want his parents to know what had happened. A new boy had come into the school and taken over Michael's group. This boy was desperate to be popular and he pushed Michael out of the

group by cleverly manipulating the other boys until they excluded Michael altogether.

Michael was devastated by the bullying. He felt he was a failure and that the bullying must somehow be his fault. Michael had never had any relationship difficulties in the past and the bullying came as a complete shock to him.

Some children and young people like Michael are suddenly thrust into a bullying situation. Others seem to be bullied constantly from the time they enter school. Is it the fault of the victims that they are bullied? In the vast majority of bullying cases, the harassment suffered by the victim is solely the fault of the bully. In a minority of cases, the victim seems to bring on the bullying.

CHRONIC VICTIMS

Some researchers say that the children who are continuously and chronically bullied may have a 'victim' mentality and even seek out ways to be bullied. An example of this is when a child, Katie, knows from past experience that saying something to another child will provoke a bullying reaction, but Katie does it anyway. Chronic victims of bullying may also be oversensitive and overreact to comments that should not bother them. Gerald was constantly getting his feelings hurt by the slightest comment, such as 'Hi, brown eyes'. His eyes were brown and this was said in an affectionate way, but Gerald somehow took offence to everything.

Your child may be a chronic victim of bullying. If so, you may recognise some of the characteristics that chronic victims like Gerald and Katie sometimes share. They:

- want any kind of attention even if it is negative
- feel that the insult or punch from the 'bully' reinforces their existing feelings that they are only worthy of bullying
- may not learn from their mistakes
- get upset if told they are good
- may destroy their own good work
- say no one likes them
- may be oversensitive
- may lack humour
- are slow to settle in
- are jumpy and wary
- are anxious
- cry easily
- have poor social skills

Obviously not every child will have all these characteristics, but children like Gerald and Katie seem to be bullied wherever they go. Changing schools in order to void a persistent bully often has little effect because they are quickly 'identified' as victims by their new classmates. The bullying then begins all over again in the new surroundings.

The chronic victim may be timid, sensitive and easily frightened. They may have been bullied for a long time before telling someone and may have come to believe much of the negative abuse hurled at them over the months/years. They react quickly and obviously to verbal abuse or physical violence by bursting into tears or blushing violently. This makes them a very satisfying target as far as the bully is concerned.

'DIFFERENT' CHILDREN

These are children who are slightly different from their fellow pupils. They may wear glasses, or a hearing aid, or have asthma, or be talented musicians, or be academically gifted – whatever the 'difference', it is enough to make them stand out from their peers. One girl was bullied because other girls were jealous of her waist-length hair.

Of course, not all children who are in some way different are bullied. But if a bully is seeking a victim, these children may come under attack.

The response of the child when first bullied is very important. Articulate, confident children may easily deflect attempts to bully them and the bully will go off to seek easier targets. However, less confident children may well be intimidated and, if the bullying persists, may eventually display some of the characteristics like low self-esteem, timidity and loneliness associated with chronic victims.

ACCIDENTAL VICTIMS

These are victims who have not been singled out particularly by the bully but who happen to be in the wrong place at the wrong time. They may become drawn into a bullying incident in which another child is the primary target, or they may be trapped by a bully or a gang of bullies just looking for someone to pick on.

SPECIAL NEEDS

Children who have an obvious physical or mental disability may be protected by most children – except the bully. They may have a disfigurement or have learning difficulties. These children make an easy target for bullies because they stand out from the crowd. Children with cerebral palsy have been bullied by comments about how they walk, children with hearing aids have been taunted, blind children have been the target of jibes and children with birthmarks have been called things like 'grape face'. All this is very hurtful and cruel.

In one case an eight-year-old boy rang KIDSCAPE's helpline to say that other children at his special needs school were bullying him because they were in wheelchairs and he was walking with sticks.

Children may also be bullied because of disabilities within their family, or because of a bereavement or divorce. One sighted girl was bullied mercilessly because both her parents were blind. Sometimes children are bullied because their parents are divorced, or because a parent has died. ('You don't have a *real* father. You haven't got a Dad.') In one case, a seven-year-old girl was constantly tormented in the playground because her father was dying of cancer and had been moved to a local hospice.

In these cases bullying can be the final straw for children who are already coping with difficult personal problems. Children can be very cruel and it is important that this sort of bullying is nipped in the bud. The victim needs to be protected from further persecution and the bullies must learn to respect other people.

RACE, RELIGION, CULTURE

Children from differing racial or cultural backgrounds may stand out in the crowd and so form easy targets for bullies. If English is not their first language, they may have difficulty in understanding everything that is said to them and may become the butt of cruel jokes.

Children should be taught that differences are not divisive but should be celebrated. The contribution made by people from different cultural, racial and religious backgrounds should be recognised and the exploration of different ideas and beliefs should be encouraged. Racial and cultural bullying is typically a product of ignorance and fear and should be challenged whenever and wherever it appears.

REASSURANCE AND PROTECTION

Whatever the reasons for the bullying of children like Michael, who was the victim of jealousy, or of Gerald and Katie, there are certain things that all victims of bullying need.

First of all, victims need reassurance. *They need to know that once they have told any adult about being bullied, they will be protected from any further bullying.* It is up to the adults involved to ensure that bullies are not given an opportunity to exact their revenge on a victim who has plucked up courage to tell. One girl who had been bullied persistently for months finally told about her ordeal. The next day she was too frightened of what the bullies would do to her to come back to school. She telephoned the headteacher to explain her fears. Far from reassuring her or promising that she would be safe, he remarked, 'Getting hurt is the risk you take when you tell.' In another case a boy told his teacher about the bullying and the teacher promised him confidentiality and worked out a way to catch the bully in the act so the boy was not further bullied for telling.

If your child has told you or a member of staff at school about bullying, ensure that your child is safe from retribution attacks by the bully or the bully's friends. You can do this by:

- insisting that the bullying is 'discovered' by an adult and that your child is not named as 'a grass'

- ensuring your child is not put at risk when going to and from school. This may mean arranging transportation or varying routes or asking that the bullies be kept behind until the other children are safely away from school

- ensuring that the school deal with the bully so that it is clear that any further attacks will lead to stringent measures and consequences

Teachers and members of staff should take responsibility for ensuring that victims do not suffer at the hands of bullies after they have told about bullying incidents.

FIGHT BACK

In the past, victims of bullying have often been told: 'Fight back', 'Learn to stand up for yourself', 'Only cowards run away', 'Don't come crying to me. You've got to learn to sort things like this out yourself'. There are still schools, organisations and families which adhere to this 'bash 'em back' mentality. The difficulty here is that most victims of bullying are not the fighting back kind of kids. Thank goodness they aren't. Don't try to make them into thugs. We've got enough thugs and bullies in the world as it is.

Telling children to fight back means that you end up with two aggressive children on your hands rather than just the original bully. Sometimes, if victims do pluck up the courage to 'fight back', they end up in trouble for provoking the fighting. If the bully is much bigger or stronger than the victim, the victim could get seriously hurt if they tried to fight the bully, especially if the bully is backed by a gang.

Pat was fed up with the bullying that had been going on for months. One day in class, the bully poked her once too often and Pat lashed out and smacked him in the face. Guess who got in trouble? Not the bully. Pat was caught and made to do detention. The bully continued to get away scot-free until Pat finally told her mother what had happened.

If a child tells about bullying, it is because they need help. If they could have sorted out the bullying by themselves, they would have done so. It is because they cannot or will not 'fight back', that they need adult support to end the bullying. Telling a bullied child to sort it out themselves is just condemning them to more of the same. It is a cop-out on the part of the adults who should be protecting and supporting the child.

We do want to teach victims how to stand up for themselves, how to be more assertive and more confident, but telling them to fight back by themselves is not an effective or positive way forward.

WAYS PARENTS CAN HELP

When your child is hurting because of bullying, there are some positive things you can do:

- encourage them to talk about their feelings
- eliminate obvious causes of bullying (smell, runny nose)
- build up low self-esteem (see chapter 4)
- teach children to cope with teasing
- make a list of what to say
- act out (roleplay) ways to cope
- practise shouting 'NO' really confidently – use a mirror
- practise walking and standing confidently – check in a mirror
- draw or write about feelings
- keep a diary of progress

TALKING

Many children who are victims of bullying feel very isolated and lonely. Taking the time to sit and talk to them can help tremendously.

Listen to what they have to say about the bullying and about why they think they are bullied. If the child has unpleasant personal habits or is dirty or smelly, talk about this and explain to the child what he/she can do to remedy the situation.

Praise them for having the courage to tell about the bullying.

Reassure them that the bullying will stop and steps will be taken to ensure that it is not repeated.

SUICIDE THREATS

I have singled this out because it is so important that we take children's threats seriously. A mother rang me to say that her eleven-year-old son had just rung her from school threatening to kill himself and what should she do. My advice was to hang up and get to the school immediately. Better safe than sorry. Children and young people do silly things when they are desperate.

There have been several very distressing cases of young people and children committing suicide because of bullying. In some cases the parents knew nothing about the problem until it was too late. In others the parents had tried to help but their child obviously had too much to cope with. My advice to parents is to watch out for any indication that your child is feeling suicidal and act to get professional help immediately.

HURTFUL COMMENTS

Teasing, discussed in chapter 1, sometimes does get out of hand. It then tips over into bullying and can be very hurtful. Some children find teasing at school devastating, even though it may have started out in a friendly sort of way.

When listening to children telling us that they have been hurt by comments, it can sometimes be tempting to dismiss the child's complaint by saying, 'It's just words – they can't hurt you.' Words do hurt and, whatever we as adults may feel, the important thing is that the child is deeply upset by what has been going on.

Some children don't know how to react to what I call 'normal' teasing; they don't know how to laugh at themselves or how to shrug off comments.

One way of helping children cope with 'normal' teasing is by teaching them low-key ways of reacting. The key is to deflect the teasing without encouraging the bully. You can help the victim by working out different responses they could make to teasing. A funny, playful response may be what the other child is expecting. Make sure your child is not overreacting to comments that are not really bullying.

However, if the teasing has become bullying, then a snappy retort or brief acknowledgement will often disconcert a bully, especially if the victim has previously responded by blushing or crying. The responses don't have to be very clever or complicated. The important thing is to encourage the victim to say something confidently back to the bully. Work out several different responses the child could make.

For example, if a child wears glasses and is being called 'Four-eyes', a quick response might be:

- 'Four eyes are better than two.'
- 'Yes, I wear glasses. I am short-sighted.'
- 'Yes, I wear glasses. So what?'
- 'Thanks' to whatever is said.

My only caution here is that sometimes children do call each other nicknames with affection. Two long-time friends of mine who have known each other since they were tiny still refer to each other as 'stinky' and 'smelly'. This really is teasing and not bullying.

Children who are called names should try not to show they are upset – bullies soon get tired of victims who never reveal their emotions. As well as practising different verbal responses to taunts, victims should also practise walking away from the bully, taking deep breaths to calm themselves down, and think assertively (see below).

However, if the name-calling is malicious and continues, then adults should step in to stop it.

COPING

When you have come up with some different ways of coping with the bullying, roleplay them with your child:

● **Practise Saying 'NO' and Walking Confidently**
The victim should practise shouting 'NO' really loudly and confidently in front of a mirror. It can really put a bully off if the formerly meek and submissive victim turns and bellows 'NO'. The victim should then walk away. They shouldn't hang about waiting for confrontation.

Your child can also practise walking 'tall'. A victim's body language can often reflect the way they feel about themselves. They may stoop, hang their heads, and hunch themselves into as small a space as possible. Practise standing up straight, holding the head high, and taking deep breaths. Stand 'like victims' and then stand 'like heroes'.

● **Draw or Write about Feelings**

Children should be encouraged to express their feelings about the bullying and about themselves through painting, writing and poems. Such activities give victims an opportunity to 'get their feelings out' and bring out their concerns. They also enable children to keep a safe distance from frightening events and emotions and give them a chance to work on ways of dealing with them.

● **Keep a Diary of Progress**

Children can keep a diary of their achievements and successes which you can read with them, if they wish. This diary should also mention times when the victim found it hard to remember or carry out the new strategies and should contain resolutions about future behaviour.

If your child is having difficulties, explain that everyone finds learning new ways of behaving difficult and that you are very proud of how hard they are trying.

● **Try Role-playing**

This is something I have used with great success in schools, and it's something you could try at home with your own children or groups of children. Act out the threatening situation and practise responding calmly but firmly. This type of activity can also help defuse some of the anger that builds up inside children who are persistently bullied.

● **Ignore that Bully**

One way that is sometimes effective in dealing with a bully is to try to completely ignore the bullying, pretend not to be upset – turn and walk quickly away. Your child may not feel confident inside, but putting on a confident front and leaving may do the trick.

● Use Humour

It is more difficult to bully a child who refuses to take the bullying seriously. This is especially useful with verbal bullying. However, it could make a situation worse if your child is being physically threatened or confronted by a large group of bullies who might become violent.

● Avoiding

It isn't fair that the bully carves out a territory, but you may have to tell your children to try to avoid places where bullying usually occurs.

● Safety in Numbers

Ask your child to stay with groups of children, if possible. Bullies usually pick on kids alone.

In order for children to feel confident using some of these ideas, you may want to help them to practise and to come up with other ideas. At the end of this chapter are a series of assertiveness exercises you may find useful to do with your children, as well.

CONFIDENCE

A few commonsense pointers which most parents will know, but I have thrown them in anyway (see also chapter 4):

- assure your children that the bullying is not their fault

- tell your children that you love them and are 100% behind them

- encourage your children to join groups outside school such as Brownies, Guides, Scouts, clubs, theatre or music groups, martial arts clubs – anything which might give them a chance to develop their talents or new friendships

- teach children relaxation techniques (below)

- invite individual children over to play

- get professional help, if necessary

Earlier in the book I talked about asking children and young people if they were being bullied. If you suspect that your child is the victim of bullying, do find out what is happening. Say, 'I think you are being bullied and I would like to hear about it.' One mother said she just went into her child's room and said, 'I m not leaving until you tell me what's happening.' After shouting and carrying on, the child did tell. Because they are often ashamed about being bullied, you may have to push them until they tell. Then you may be able to help by using some of the suggestions in this chapter.

ASSERTIVENESS TRAINING EXERCISES
These exercises are designed to introduce children to new ways of behaving which will give them strategies for coping with bullying and with other difficult situations.

They also teach children to think differently about themselves by giving *themselves* praise and encouragement.

Some of these exercises are designed to be used with more than one child, so you can pretend to be the other child if you are using this at home with your child.

MAKING A REQUEST

First of all, explain that there are three basic rules when making a request:

1. **Be clear about what you want**
2. **Make your request short** (for example, 'That is my pencil. I would like it back, please')
3. **Plan and practise** (even if you just go over the request in your own mind)

You have to decide what you are going to say and then stick to it. ('That is my pencil. I want it back.') Don't allow yourself to be sidetracked away from the main issue: it is your pencil and you want it back.

SAY NO

If someone is asking you for something which you don't want to agree to, you have the right to say no. It is not selfish to say no and there are occasions when saying no is right for you.

Again, decide what you are going to say and stick to it. Be kind but firm. 'I am sorry that you don't have a pencil but I don't want to lend my pencil.'

Don't get sidetracked into apologising for your decision or justifying it. Don't make excuses. Keep your body assertive, don't smile and keep good eye contact. (Sometimes shy children are bad at making eye contact – get them to practise with their families.)

If you are not sure what to say, listen to your body and feelings. What do you really want to do? What do you really want to say? You could say something like 'I'm not sure. I need more time/more information to decide.'

You can offer an alternative: 'No, I don't want to play football. Let's go for a walk instead.'

When you say 'No' say it early, if possible first.

BROKEN RECORD

In this exercise, children practise saying the same thing over and over again like a broken record. This is a technique which can be used if someone is trying to get round you, or if you are not being listened to, or for saying no.

Ask your child to pretend that she or he has a new bicycle and you want to borrow it. Your child doesn't want anyone to play with the new bike. You keep trying to get the bike from your child. Tell your child not to give in and to resist you taking the bicycle. Of course we are talking about using words, not fists! Try it for about a minute.

Repeat the exercise but this time have your child try to borrow your new football or computer game.

FOGGING

If we respond to insults with more insults, it builds up. We do not need to do this – we can 'fog'. Fogging swallows up insults like a great fog-bank swallows sights and sounds.

When other people make hurtful remarks, we don't have to argue or become upset; we can turn ourselves into fog and swallow up what they say. If it's true, we respond 'That's right'. If it's not true, we respond 'You could be right' or 'It's possible'. Don't take the insult personally and keep the answers short and bland.

This may seem very strange at first, but fogging offers an alternative to distress or violence.

RELAXATION

Tense and unhappy children can find it very hard to relax and it is a good idea to teach them the following simple exercise.

Ask your child to lie on the floor. Ask the child to tense every muscle until they feel really rigid. Then ask the child slowly to relax their muscles, starting with their toes and gradually working up to their head. At the end they should be floppy like a rag doll.

WAYS OF LEARNING ASSERTIVENESS

Help children learn to be assertive by giving them the chance to practise the new skills in a safe and supportive atmosphere.

Ask them 'what if' questions. (What would you do if a bully came up to you in the playground and started calling you names? What would you do if a bully cornered you in the lavatories and asked for your money?) You can help them work out the best course of action and they can practise different responses.

Talk about situations the child finds difficult. Teach them that they cannot change what has happened in the past but they can learn from it. Discuss particular incidents with the child. Could they have behaved differently? Said or done something else? Would it have made the situation better or worse? Discuss what they could do if the same thing happened again. Discuss different strategies and ways of coping which are possible for the child and practise them in roleplays.

Some victims have poor posture and tend to creep about. They need to learn how to stand up straight, how to walk confidently, how to make and keep eye contact. Get them to practise in front of a mirror.

They need to learn how other people behave. Get the child to pretend to be a detective. They should watch other people, look at eye contact, look at the way people stand, the way they walk, listen to their tone of voice, listen to what they say. Ask them to decide what is passive, what is aggressive and what is assertive behaviour. They could write a report on someone they have been studying. (Warn them not to stare bug-eyed at some unsuspecting acquaintance!)

WHAT IF? QUESTIONS

It may help to get your child to think in advance about what he or she might do if a bullying situation arose.

There are no 'right' answers because every case is different. Use the questions with your children and ask them what they think might work? They could also think of their own solutions and you can make up new What If? questions to answer.

How to Help Victims

1. You are walking to school and a gang of older bullies demands your money, skateboard, trainers, etc. Do you:
   a. Fight them?
   b. Shout and run away?
   c. Give them the money?

   * Give them the money (or other possessions) – your safety is more important than money.

2. You are on the school playground and someone accidentally trips you. Do you:
   a. Hit the person hard?
   b. Give him or her a chance to apologise?
   c. Sit down and cry?

   * Give the person a chance. If it was an accident, then he or she should say sorry.

3. You are in the school toilet and an older student comes in, punches you and then tells you not to do anything or 'you'll get worse'. You know who the person is and you have never done anything to him/her. Do you:
   a. Wait until the person leaves and then tell a teacher?
   b. Get in a fight with him/her?
   c. Accept what happened and don't tell?

   * You didn't deserve to be punched and the bully was wrong to do it. If you don't tell, the bully will just keep on beating up other kids.

4. You are walking into the lunch room and someone yells out a negative comment directed at you. Do you:
   a. Ignore it?

45

b. Yell back?

c. Tell?

* You can either ignore it (if it is the first time and that's all that happened) or tell if it really bothers you.

5. A gang of bullies gets you alone and starts beating you. Do you:

a. Do nothing – just take it?

b. Fight back?

c. Shout to attract attention?

d. Watch for your chance and run away?

* You must decide, but answers (c) and (d) together would work very well. It would be quite difficult to fight a whole gang of bullies and you might be badly hurt if you did.

6. Someone in your class makes rude comments about you and says them loud enough for you (and others) to hear. It really upsets you. Do you?

a. Ignore the comments?

b. Confront the bully and tell him/her off?

c. Tell the teacher?

d. Punch the bully in the nose?

* You may feel like punching the bully in the nose but you'll probably get into trouble if you do. Try answer (a) first – ignoring comments is difficult, but can work if the bully gets tired of trying to get you to be angry or cry or show some reaction. Your teacher should be told about the comments. If you are feeling brave, tell the bully off. Try practising in the mirror to get the right effect!

7. You see someone being bullied. Do you:
   a. Ignore it, walk by and be thankful it isn't you?
   b. Stop the bully?
   c. Get help?

   * Ignoring the bully is cowardly and unfair to the victim. You can try to stop it, if you can do so without getting hurt. Perhaps getting several other children to stop it would work. At the very least, yell at the victim that you are getting help and get a teacher or other adult to intervene.

8. Your former 'best' friends start to bully you. This hurts your feelings and you are quite miserable. Do you:
   a. Tell your parents?
   b. Do nothing?
   c. Ring one member of the group and ask why they are doing this?
   d. Try to find a new group?

   * Talk to your parents and try to ring one or two members of the group to see if you can stop their behaviour. It sometimes works to have the parents, if they are friends, talk to each other. You can also try to find a new group because this group may not be worth having as friends if they are so cruel to you.

9. Your friend's dad recently died and some students are saying and making hurtful comments about it. Do you:
   a. Come to his defence and tell them to stop it?

    b. Ignore it, it will stop eventually?
    c. Let the teacher know?

    * Do come to his defence and tell the bullies that their comments aren't funny. Also let the teacher know so that he/she can talk about death and address the fears of the bullying children about their own parents dying. This is why they are making comments in the first place.

10. A new student comes into your class in the middle of the year and some students are bullying him/her. Do you:
    a. Make an effort to be friendly and invite him/her to eat lunch with you and your friends?
    b. Join in the bullying?
    c. Ignore it – everyone gets bullied at first, so don't join in, but don't help the new student either?

    * Remember how hard it is to be new, and do everything you can to make the new student feel welcome by inviting him/her to join in with you. If you see that the new student is being bullied, do tell the teacher.

11. Your friends tell you to skip school or they will bully you. Do you:
    a. Go along with them?
    b. Stay in school?
    c. Get them in trouble by telling on them?

    * They aren't really your friends if they want to get you into trouble and threaten to bully you. Don't go!

How to Help Victims

12. Someone you know is being bullied because they are fat (spotty, small, wear glasses, are disabled, have red hair, don't like football, etc.). Do you:
    a. Stand up for them?
    b. Join in?
    c. Let adults know what is happening?

    * They can't help what they are and no one deserves to be bullied because they are different. Stand up for them and tell your parents and the teacher what is happening.

13. Some students in your school make racist comments to minority groups. Do you:
    a. Ignore it and don't get involved?
    b. Enlist the help of other students and teachers to stop the bullies making these comments?
    c. Hit the kids making comments?

    * Racist comments are wrong and hurtful. Everyone has the right to their own culture and religion. Try answer (b).

14. Someone you know is a bully. Do you:
    a. Try to find out why?
    b. Bully him/her?
    c. Try being a friend and setting a good example?

    * If the bully is someone you can help, try being a friend. The bully may not know how to act properly. Bullies are sometimes quite unhappy and need adult help and counselling to sort out their problem.

15. An adult is bullying you. Do you:
    a. Say nothing?
    b. Tell another adult you trust?
    c. Get some students together and tell the adult to stop?

    * This is very difficult for children. Best to try to get another adult to help.

16. You see someone being badly beaten on a bus/Tube. Do you:
    a. Get off at the next stop?
    b. Help the victim?
    c. Tell the conductor/guard or driver?
    d. Pull the emergency cord?

    * If you can help, do so. Also, tell someone in charge. If you can get no help and the person is being badly hurt, pull the emergency cord or push a button when the train comes into the station.

17. A bully has threatened your little brother. He has begged you not to tell your parents. Do you:
    a. Tell him to handle it?
    b. Confront the bully?
    c. Tell your parents?

    * Your brother cannot handle it or he wouldn't have told you. If you confront the bully, the bully might get a gang together against you. Talk to your brother and see if he'll come home with you to tell your parents, because they should know so they can help.

POINTS TO REMEMBER

If you find out that your child is being bullied:

1. Don't ignore the problem.

2. Encourage your child to talk to you about his/her feelings – tell your child you are always willing to listen.

3. Try not to overreact, even if you are furious – it might frighten your child into silence and we want victims to talk, not retreat.

4. Ask your child if he or she has any suggestions about changing the situation.

5. Find out how fearful your child is and make sure that he or she feels protected.

6. Take any threats of suicide or other desperate pleas seriously and seek help – better safe than sorry and children and young people sometimes go to extremes if they are miserable.

7. Help your child develop a sense of humour as a way of 'throwing off' taunts.

8. Praise your child, tell him/her how much you love and support them.

9. Try to sort out the bullying at first as quietly and constructively as possible:

-   Contact class teacher.

-   Try to give the situation time to change.

-   If there is no improvement, contact the head-teacher.

-   If you are still concerned, contact school governors – the school can tell you how to do this.

-   If your child is still not being helped, then contact your Local Education Authority (LEA).

-   If you feel confident enough, you may wish to contact the parents of the other child – that obviously depends upon the family of the bully. There are some families which bully not only their own children, but threaten anyone who comes near them – best to check out the situation carefully before getting involved.

-   If you feel that your child needs legal advice, contact the Children's Legal Centre.

-   If your child has been injured or threatened, you can contact the police.

10. Encourage your child to develop new interests which might lead to a supportive group of friends

– in school and out of school – as well as new skills. Saturday music clubs, church choir, sports activities, local drama groups, dancing/art/computer classes, confidence-building courses like Quindo, Ki Aikido non-aggressive self-defence, Red Cross training, etc. – all of these could improve self-confidence and give an opportunity to meet new people. Local councils and libraries will be able to give you an idea of what is available.

3

HOW TO HELP BULLIES

Darren aged eight had become the scourge of the neighbourhood. He was bullying children left, right and centre. His parents had been rung by the neighbours so many times that they lost count. They were in despair. They tried hitting Darren, yelling at him, taking away his pocket money, all to no avail. When his parents contacted me, Darren was well on the way to being the child from hell. Interestingly Darren did not act up at school because the school had strict anti-bullying policies. The first time Darren tried to bully someone else he found out the school wasn't kidding. There were immediate consequences and Darren decided that it wasn't worth the trouble.

So what was the school doing that Darren's parents could learn from? The first thing the school did was to lay down the ground rules and what would happen if you broke the rules. Everyone knew what was what.

Unfortunately, Darren's parents were more erratic. Darren never knew what would happen – he knew something would happen, but it seemed worth the risk. In fact, occasionally his parents ignored his behaviour. After meeting with Darren and his parents, we decided on a course of action. Darren had to learn how to get on with children, so we roleplayed the right way to act and what to do if he was provoked. We also worked through some of the What If? questions listed in the

chapter on How to Help Victims to try to help him develop empathy.

The first thing Darren's parents needed to do was to talk to the neighbours and tell them that they were working to ensure that the bullying behaviour stopped. They asked the neighbours to tell them immediately if Darren bullied their children.

Then Darren's parents had a talk with Darren when they were calm and before anything happened again. They told him that they did not expect him to bully people and that if he did, he would be staying at home and not be allowed to go out in the neighbourhood for that day. He would be allowed to go out the next day to try to be nice. But every time he bullied he would be back in the house. The hitting as punishment was stopped. It had not helped and probably made it worse since Darren was furious about being hit and took out his anger on the other kids.

Darren's parents also asked him to explain what happened that led up to the bullying. The other kids teased Darren about his ears and when they did, he blew his top. Darren and his parents thought it would be good if Darren could just ignore the taunting and walk away. In the meantime, his parents would let the other parents know about the remarks being made.

They also decided that Darren could try asking one boy, who seemed to like Darren, over to play some games and then bring in the other children little by little.

Eventually Darren stopped bullying because he felt more confident, and the other children stopped making fun of him. His parents were better able to cope because they handled the situation when there was no heat or anger. Darren understood exactly where he stood and what would happen if he transgressed. And Darren's parents were able to help him because they understood his hurt feelings about the taunting.

There are many reasons a child or young person might bully others. Dan Olweus found in his long-term studies that children who bully can be high-spirited, active, energetic children. They may be easily bored or envious or insecure. They may also be secure children who just like getting their own way and who may have become 'heroes' with the other children for the way they behave. They may be spoilt brats, over-indulged and undisciplined.

Bullies might also be jealous of another's academic or sporting success, or they may be jealous of a sibling or new baby. They may have a learning disability which makes them angry and frustrated (though this may have the opposite effect and make them a target for bullies instead).

As parents we should keep in mind that most children throw their weight around and pick on others at some time. It is an unacceptable behaviour and we usually nip it in the bud by admonishment or sanctions such as losing privileges, but sometimes it gets out of hand. That is when parents need to take strong and immediate action if we are to prevent our children from becoming unmanageable thugs.

OCCASIONAL BULLIES

Once in a while a child will lash out and suddenly start bullying. It is quite possible that the reason this is happening is because the child was being bullied and could stand it no longer. Unfortunately when this happens, the child is labelled a bully when the child really has been a victim. Be very careful not to start blaming your child until you have all the facts about why he or she has mysteriously turned into a bully. It may also be that the child is having a 'bad day', or is unmindful that what they are doing is bullying.

Think about the possible reasons why children may behave in this way. They may be:

- jealous of brother or sister or other children
- under stress because of school work or exam pressure
- worried about a problem that's cropped up at home, such as a pet dying, parents fighting or separating, a favourite sibling leaving home, a bereavement or money problems
- quarrelling with a friend – they might vent their anger on someone else
- bored
- frustrated – learning or language difficulties
- everything gone wrong type of day

Any of these difficulties might trigger bullying behaviour in a child who normally behaves well with other children. The bottom line is that a child who bullies only once and very occasionally is not difficult to help. Of course, they need firm guidelines and telling off, and they need to make amends for their behaviour. But we don't need to beat our parental breasts and feel terrible that we have produced a 'bully'.

If you find your child has been in trouble for this kind of bullying and are in despair over what to do, try:

1. to remain calm and in control
2. to find out all the facts, including the actions of the other children involved
3. to discuss the problem with the child – it may help just to talk it over

4. to find out if your child is upset, worried, jealous, unhappy or perhaps has been bullied
5. to find out if your child knows what harm she or he is causing by acting this way
6. to sort things out with the parents of the victim, so that the bullying does not escalate
7. to see the school staff and to offer your help and support to them. Arrange regular reports from them so you all know that your child is back on track
8. to emphasise that bullying is not acceptable in any circumstances and that you will not tolerate it
9. to give your child some goals to behave better and then reward good behaviour
10. to help your child learn how to be a friend to others. Perhaps you could invite over some children and make sure the visit is fun for all
11. to work out some alternative ways the child could react if the situation occurs again, such as:
    ● going to a 'time-out' room in which to cool off
    ● walking away
    ● deep breathing
    ● counting to ten
12. to give your child plenty of praise and encouragement if they don't repeat the bullying and are able to use some of the alternative responses
13. to determine if your child needs help coping with a crisis like a parental divorce or the death of someone they loved. He or she may need emotional support, like someone outside the family to talk to, or professional counselling.

CHRONIC BULLIES

Some children go from incident to incident, from school to school, bullying and hurting others. These children may eventually end up being excluded from mainstream education if they continue with this behaviour. Many of these children have some characteristics or backgrounds in common. They may:

- act aggressively much of the time
- be unable to control themselves
- have a positive attitude towards violence
- feel insecure
- be disruptive
- blame the victims for the bullying (i.e. 'He looked at me funny – deserved to be thumped')
- have no empathy with anyone
- be bullied by family members
- be scapegoats in the family (i.e. blamed for everything, even if it isn't their fault)
- feel under tremendous pressure to succeed when, in fact, they are failing
- have poor social skills
- feel different, stupid or inadequate
- come from a 'culture of violence' in the home

Chronic bullies may also be over-indulged to the point of being worshipped by their parents, and expect that everyone should bow to their wishes. Hopefully your child is not a chronic bully, but if he or she is, there are some things you can do to help.

If we as parents can recognise that these chronic bullies may be victims in many ways (perhaps unloved or mistreated, or covering up for a feeling of personal inadequacy by dominating others), then we can begin to undo the damage. In these cases, treating the underlying cause may also eradicate the bullying. For example, a child with an otherwise poor school record who is encouraged to work hard and excel at some particular subject – art, photography, computing – may in the process gain enough approval to stop bullying.

It does help if parents of the bullied children can take a sympathetic approach towards the parents of the bully – acknowledging that any of us could find ourselves a parent of a bully one day. There is more likely to be progress this way than if the parents of the bully are ostracised and hated. In practice, this sort of bridge-building between the parents of the victims and the parents of bullies is not always possible. But it may work, especially in the case of over-indulged, self-satisfied bullies, if those parents wake up and realise their 'little darlings' are really 'little devils'. But, in general, knowing that bullies may be actually self-hating or unhappy or spoilt will be of small comfort to the mother of a bullied child.

Keep in mind that reforming the behaviour of a chronic bully is not easy; power may be the only language they understand. Significantly, when schools organise meetings to discuss the problem of bullying, it is usually the parents of the victim who turn up.

CHANGING THE BULLY'S BEHAVIOUR

Once you have dealt with the immediate fall-out from the latest bullying incident, you are ready to begin on the long-term task of helping your child change so that he or she develops other non-bullying ways of behaving and reacting. This is a lengthy, time-consuming process with no guarantees of success, but a committed parent can make all the difference.

Peer pressure is, of course, one of the most effective ways of stamping out bullying. A strong peer leader can ensure that bullying does not happen. But children may only outlaw bullying amongst themselves after long discussions, role-plays, drawing up and signing contracts, and understanding what is and what is not acceptable behaviour between individuals and groups. This can only happen in the context of the school, so you certainly will want to enlist their help (see chapter 6).

There are no definitive solutions or strategies for changing a bully's behaviour which *always* work. Each bully is an individual with his or her own problems and there is no general 'cure' for bullying. However, guidelines as to what has worked with bullies elsewhere can be helpful.

1. Set the rules

Discuss with the child the behaviour which you expect. Give them clear guidelines as to their future behaviour. This will help to eliminate any future misunderstandings. (e.g. 'If you do this again, then you will have your pocket money cut' or 'If you behave, then you will be allowed more pocket money or a treat of some kind.')

2. *Admit, Acknowledge, Apologise, Atone*

Before you can begin to change your child's behaviour, your child has to *admit* that what they have done is wrong. They must *acknowledge* that their behaviour has been hurtful and unkind.

They have to realise that they owe the victim an *apology* and they should try to *atone* for what they have done. The child may apologise, however grudgingly, and hand back stolen items or money, without feeling any remorse, only anger that they have been 'found out'. This does not mean the apology is meaningless. It is merely a starting point and is one way of bringing home to your child that what they have done is wrong and unacceptable.

3. *Set short-term goals*

Discuss the next steps with your child and set realistic short-term goals. Make sure that these goals are attainable, even if you set something like 'No bullying for the day or morning', or even for thirty minutes if the child has little control. Work something out with the school, as well as at home. It is better to give a child an easy target, even if you think it ludicrously simple, thus virtually guaranteeing success, rather than set them a hard task which a child might fail and which might be discouraging and unrealistic.

4. *Break the pattern*

If your child is often involved in bullying incidents, find out if there is a pattern to the bullying. It would be helpful to keep a record of every bullying incident, if possible.

- How long has the bullying been going on?

- Do particular situations provoke your child?

- Is there just one victim or does your child target several children?

The answers to these questions will help you identify what triggers bullying in your child. Perhaps the bullying happens at lunch with one child because your child can't stand the fact the victim is more popular than he or she is. In this circumstance you may be able to work with the teachers and lunch-room supervisors to either make sure the children are not at the same table or that they don't eat at the same time. Obviously you would also need to work on ensuring that your child overcame his or her jealousy of the other child. That might happen if you start helping your child develop more social skills, perhaps by roleplaying how he or she should act.

You could also, depending upon the age of your child, arrange for children to come over on an individual basis and ensure that they have a good time and feel kindly towards your child. That might give him or her more people to eat lunch with, thus partly solving that problem.

5. Teach good social skills

Draw up some clear behaviour guidelines on how you expect your child to behave in future. If your child does not seem to know acceptable ways of behaving, he or she may need some very basic information about generally accepted standards of behaviour. (e.g. 'When you talk to other people, you smile, look them in the eyes and act in a pleasant manner. Now let's try it. You pretend that I am someone you have met or want to eat lunch with.' Then act out the parts and praise your child for getting it right.)

6. Raise self-esteem

If your child has very low self-esteem, as may be the case with children who are bullies, you need to work on improving their self-image (see chapter 4). Give your child extra responsibilities. Increase responsibility gradually, otherwise children might panic because they feel they can't cope. Give them plenty of praise and encouragement when they behave well or complete tasks successfully. Help them build up their self-respect. They won't learn to respect others until they have learned to respect themselves.

7. Plan useful activities

If your child is active, boisterous, quick-tempered, you need to divert that excess energy into useful activities. Get them to help with physical tasks – fetching and carrying jobs, painting a wall, tidying rooms, cooking, going on errands, planting flowers in the garden or in pots or on the balcony, walking the dog, setting the table – basically anything that gets them moving in a positive way. Give them lots of praise and/or rewards. Suggest to the teacher that they may want to do the same at school – ask the child to get equipment ready, put out chairs, stack books, put up displays, etc. This way you and the teacher might get lots of help and your child is so busy there is no time to bully! Don't give them sedentary tasks – they'll just get frustrated and perhaps be twice as unruly afterwards.

8. *Discourage fighting*

If your child is aggressive and often involved in fights at school, ask the teacher to set a short-term goal such as 'No fighting this morning'. Suggest that, if they get through the morning without fighting, the teacher could praise them and give them a reward – five minutes extra at break, perhaps. Get them to keep a diary of their progress. Keep reminding them of the goal. Gradually extend the time period ('No fighting today, tomorrow, this week') as the child learns to control his or her actions and learns different ways of reacting to difficult situations.

Be prepared for setbacks and for discouragement. Keeping a bully motivated is often very difficult and you will need all your reserves of patience and persistence!

9. *Freeze the action*

Discuss with your child what sort of situations make him or her flare up and then help them find other ways of reacting. Make up some simple roleplays based on what the bully has told you. Have your child play him or herself and 'freeze' the action at the point where your child usually lashes out or starts challenging others – think about other ways of behaving: walking away, deep breathing, going to a 'time-out room' to cool off.

10. *Assertive vs aggressive*

Teach your child the difference between aggressive and assertive behaviour. Work out verbal responses which are assertive rather than aggressive. For example, 'Turn off that horrible music NOW' could be replaced with 'Would you mind please turning off that music – it bothers me while I'm working.' I am sure most parents would recognise themselves in that quote – at least I have certainly heard myself saying aggressively to my children, 'TURN THAT BLASTED MUSIC DOWN!' Perhaps our children are sometimes repeating what they hear from us?

Anyway, teaching children to be assertive instead of aggressive does help.

11. *Give encouragement*

Encourage your child to persist with 'behaviour-changing' programmes by giving lots of praise and rewards for good behaviour. It is a lot of work, but it is worth it.

12. *Don't spoil*

If you recognise that your child is a bully because they are 'spoilt' at home, change your behaviour and tell your child why. It will be traumatic, but it has to be done. One way to start is by getting your child to do some sort of community service with you such as helping out in a soup kitchen. The realisation that not everyone has been as indulged as he or she might bring about some enlightenment.

13. *Make them aware*

In the event that your child does not know or understand about the pain and suffering their actions cause their victims, give them a copy of the Letter from the Bully at the end of this chapter and discuss it with them. Get them to write a similar letter. Make up a series of What If? questions to help make your child aware of how bullying affects people.

You can use roleplays to give your child a chance to empathise with victims. Get your child to play the victim and ask them to discuss how they feel in this role. Of course if your child is a bully because they have been bullied, this would not be appropriate unless it was used to help them get out pent-up feelings. It should be used with care.

14. *Help relieve frustration*

If your child is frustrated and angry because of learning difficulties or some other problem, remedial tuition, extra coaching or counselling should be arranged.

15. *Seek professional help*

If your child is suffering through a divorce or bereavement, he or she may need emotional support and professional counselling.

16. *Seek medical help*

It may be that your child has a medical condition such as hyperactivity, which could be helped by your GP.

17. *Organise supervision*

Your child may need increased supervision. See if the school can help by assigning a teacher or another staff member to the bully. This could be a pastoral member of staff, or someone the child particularly likes (or who likes the child!). This person will act as a safety-valve for your child – someone they can talk to if they feel a bullying incident 'coming on'. This may be difficult with staff overburdened by work and time pressures, but it can be extremely helpful for your child to have a 'friend' they can approach for support.

One mother decided to supervise her child herself. With the co-operation of the school, she sat in on his classes and watched him on the playground and in the lunch room. The boy vowed after one day of this that he would never bully anyone again.

Make sure all members of staff including playground supervisors, catering staff, and bus escort know that your child is trying to change their behaviour. Ask them to keep an eye on the child and to be aware of their activities. They should be ready to step in if the bully becomes embroiled in difficult or hostile situations.

18. Pressure to bully

Sometimes, if children know that a bully is trying to 'reform', they will try to provoke the bully into displaying their old, aggressive behaviour and will tease and taunt the bully until he or she loses control and reacts angrily. Parents and school staff should be on the look-out for this sort of baiting. They should also beware of making comments like, 'Look out, here comes trouble'. This sort of remark indicates to those around your child and to your child, that aggressive, bullying behaviour is expected of them and seems to exclude the possibility that they might behave in any other way.

19. Set an example

One of the best ways to help children to change their behaviour is by setting an example of the right way to behave towards other people. If your child sees you or members of staff at school shouting, using sarcasm as a weapon, and picking on people, they will assume that, whatever anybody says to them, bullying is OK. Why should they then change their behaviour?

20. *No instant results*

Do not expect instant results. It can take anything from six months to two years to change a persistent bully's behaviour and there are likely to be setbacks along the way. The older the child, the harder it is to change ingrained behaviour patterns, but every parent knows you have to try if your child is acting this way because we know that young bullies grow up to be big bullies. And none of us wants that.

I WAS THE SCHOOL BULLY

I don't really know how to explain things. I never even realised how awful I was at school until I was at least twenty-two. One day one of the managers at work told me that his daughter had been at the same school as me. She used to dread meeting me at school and she said that I was well known as the school bully. I'd never really admitted to myself that what I did was bullying – it was just a bit of fun as far as I was concerned. I was embarrassed that the manager talked to me. I wanted to drop through the floor. But it made me think about what I had done all those years ago.

It's not that my childhood was so awful. Yes, my parents were always fighting, and my brother picked on me all the time. But I guess lots of kids have stories like that to tell about their lives. I really didn't have much excuse to do what I did, but I liked the feeling of power that bullying gave me. No one messed with me!

I think the bullying started when somebody upset me in the Infants and some of the boys showed me how to make a fist and 'sort her out'. I suppose I just carried on from there. I never used a gang for support and I picked on boys and girls – it didn't matter who they were. I'd lie in wait for them on the way home. I used to catcall and fight them – not just pulling hair and scratching but real fighting. I even knocked a girl out once. I was never beaten. Perhaps I would have stopped if somebody had been able to beat me.

I always had an excuse for why I bullied. Things like, 'they were snobs' or 'they'd hurt me' but I know they were pathetic excuses. The lads used to egg me on as well but even when we moved to another area I still carried on. The bullying went on until I left school.

I used to feel a rush whenever I got at someone. I seemed to get satisfaction from knowing that I'd hurt and beaten others. At heart, I was scared. I thought nobody liked me. I thought I was ugly. I had a big nose and the boys all used to tease me. I felt very insecure about how I looked, but then again lots of people feel that way and never bully others.

I am writing to you in the hopes that some young bully might read this and change his or her ways before it is too late. Now I feel really bad about what I did, but I wonder if any of my victims will ever know?

POINTS TO REMEMBER

If you find your child has been bullying other children:

1. Ask your child if she or he can explain what has happened and why – try not to be too judgemental at this point.

2. Talk with your child and find out if there are ways you can work together to stop his or her behaviour.

3. Explain that the bullying must stop and that the situation could become worse if it doesn't (the possibility that the child might be suspended from school or that police action might have to be taken in serious cases should be discussed, if appropriate).

4. Explain how frightening the bullying is for the victim and try to encourage empathy.

5. Criticise the bullying behaviour, but don't reject your child or label him or her as a 'bully'. ('What you did was wrong' instead of 'You are a terrible person' or 'You're a bully.)

6. Look for good behaviour from your child and praise it, even if it is something small like closing the door without slamming it or picking up clothes and putting them away.

7. Tell your child you know he or she can change the bullying behaviour – say that you know the child is NOT really a bully. Give your child the confidence to try to change.

8. If possible help your child to develop new interests and/or friends away from the 'bully gang'. Work on improving social skills – how to approach people, how to say nice things, how not to react if she or he is angry.

9. Try to spend as much time with your child as you can, especially listening to his or her concerns. Sometimes children bully other children as a way of getting attention.

10. Make it clear that you do not accept bullying behaviour and that there will be consequences at home such as no television or loss of privileges if the bullying does not stop.

4

BUILDING SELF-ESTEEM

Fifteen-year-old Mark was a mass of nerves. He had been bullied ever since entering secondary school. Whenever the boys who bullied him came up to him, Mark automatically went into victim mode. He felt he must have done something to deserve what was happening, even if he didn't have a clue about what it was. He was self-critical when the bullies said Mark was stupid and a jerk and why didn't he just jump off a bridge. He said nothing when they tore up his homework, took his lunch money and stole his jacket. Mark had no self-esteem and no self-confidence. He may have had both at some time in his life, but the bullies had destroyed whatever he had.

It was possible to restore some of Mark's battered self-esteem, but he has not yet managed to shake off the feeling that perhaps he was bullied because there was something the matter with him. The reality is that the bullies needed a victim and Mark proved to be perfect.

The bullies had previously tried to harass Julian, but Julian did not react and told them to get lost (well, he said something else I can't print, but you get the idea). Basically Julian was full of confidence and did not think he should have to put up with the way the bullies tried to treat him.

WHAT IS IT?

What is self-esteem? It is how we feel about ourselves. People with good self-esteem like themselves. No one is born with bad feelings about themselves. Children who feel bad about themselves have got the message that somehow they are unlovable or not worth much. Sometimes these messages come from parents and family members, sometimes they come from other people such as teachers, children or acquaintances.

Fostering self-esteem in children is one of the most important tasks we have as parents. Repairing the self-esteem of children like Mark is much harder than building self-esteem in young children. There is hope for Mark, however. Although we can't undo the damage that has been done, we can go from here to develop trust, new skills, new friends and let Mark know that he is loved unconditionally – no strings attached. (See Strategies for Repair.)

Have you ever wondered why some children seem to develop into self-confident people? I remember one mother saying to me, 'Jane is so popular and funny, if only my Belinda were like that.' It isn't always the brightest who succeed in this way, or those born into families with power and influence. We only have to look to certain members of society who are constantly in trouble with the law for drugs, drink or driving offences or even alleged murder to know that just having money or privileges or even being intelligent counts for very little if you have no self-esteem.

There are some ways we can help our children to become self-confident from a very early age:

1. Use praise

'Clever girl!' Three-year-old Marie's mother scoops up her daughter and gives her a big hug. Marie giggles excitedly. What has brought about this jubilation? Marie has 'cleaned' her room. Never mind that it still looks a mess to a critical eye. Marie's mother knows that Marie has tried her best and she is not being critical. Marie feels proud of her achievement and her mother is starting her on the road to self-esteem.

When seven-year-old Richard missed an important goal and felt really terrible, his father's comment was, 'Never mind, there's always a next time and you did your best.' Richard still wished he had made the goal, but knew that his dad had faith in him.

School results for thirteen-year-old Beth were not as good as she hoped, but she and her parents knew that she hadn't given it her best effort. In fact, there had been angry words about how her study habits took second place to her desire to go out with friends and talk on the telephone. Beth was depressed about the results and her parents wanted to say 'told you so'. Nevertheless, her parents bit their tongues and said, 'We know you aren't happy with what you've done, but we believe you can do better. How can we work together to make sure this doesn't happen again?' At least they were giving Beth the message that they knew she had it in her to do better instead of telling her that she was a failure.

Children who feel good about themselves are much more likely to be successful in relationships with other children. I think that building self-esteem is one of the most important things we can do for children and we can start from the moment they give us that first smile. When we smile back and say to our babies that they are the best and most beautiful creatures on earth (even if it was just a burp that produced that smile), they don't understand the words, but they soon get the idea that we think they are wonderful. Having parents who think you are the cat's meow is the first step in building self-esteem. Other people will play a big part in building your children's self-esteem, but none will play as great a role as you.

Your children's feelings about themselves will shape their entire lives. It will influence how they do in school, who their friends are, who they marry, what kind of parents they will be, the jobs they will try for and the way they will look at the world. Self-esteem, in my opinion, is vital for children.

Of course, we will need to make sure that our children don't turn into insufferable little monsters with egos the size of the moon. Our delight in them and praise for them will need to be tempered with good sense and limits or we will end up with the spoilt brat bullies discussed in chapter 3. What we want is a child with self-esteem who is ready to try anything (within reason).

2. Words of encouragement

Children need to know that we are behind them and that we think they can do well. Children will try lots of things. Sometimes they'll succeed, sometimes they'll fail. What can we say to help?

Try using some of the following messages with your children. They may seem obvious, but too often we forget to praise, but remember to criticise.

O   PRAISE FOR ACHIEVEMENT
   ● Awesome
   ● Brilliant
   ● I'm very impressed

- You've got it!
- Well done
- I'm so proud of you and what you've done
- Clever girl/boy
- Fantastic
- You deserve to be very proud
- You're a winner
- You're a star
- You're first rate – couldn't be better
- Marvellous achievement
- You've outdone yourself
- I'm so proud that you're my son/daughter

○ WHEN SOMETHING DOESN'T WORK OUT
- Good try, I'm proud of you
- That was a great improvement
- You're doing much better
- Excellent effort
- I can tell you've been practising
- You're getting the idea
- You really stuck to that
- You've come such a long way
- Every day it's getting better and better
- Things take time, don't be discouraged
- Rome wasn't built in a day (my grandmother always said this)
- You're learning a lot
- You did your best
- You tried hard – I am so pleased

I am sure that you have a million things you could say – these are just to get you going. Praise works wonders to build self-esteem. Try it!

3. Give them lots of experiences

In order to develop self-esteem, children need to find out those things that they can do well in and which excite them. Then they try things out, find they succeed and their self-confidence and esteem grow.

Children's horizons will be expanded if they have the opportunity to experience as many different activities and interests as possible. By taking the effort to get your children to as many different places and activities as you can – exhibitions, museums, plays, cinemas, concerts, railway journeys, sports events and anything else you can think of – you will increase their appreciation of life's experiences. Although many children get information about the world from television and though much of that information is excellent, television is a poor substitute for actual experience.

When Louise took her six-year-old daughter, Sara, to a concert for the first time, she was amazed that the little girl thought music came from tape cassettes. She really did not know that people played the instruments. 'I just assumed that somewhere along the way she would have realised this,' said Louise. 'The good thing is that she now wants to try an instrument, though I do think the trombone is too long for her arms.' Instead Louise started Sara taking violin lessons and Sara will be giving her own first concert in a few months. Sara is full of confidence about music and full of confidence in her own abilities.

What we as parents are doing is giving our children a variety of things which might inspire them to try something new and different, which could give them another opportunity to shine and to develop a new skill, and thus more self-esteem.

William, who was badly bullied for six months at school, has been helped by his father taking a particular interest in opening up his son's eyes to the many things he can do. William is starting to feel that he is worthwhile, and perhaps the bully, not William, is the problem, after all. His father started by spending time taking William to the local swimming bath to teach him to swim. They then joined a martial arts class. 'It's not that I want William to bash anyone,' said his dad, 'it's just that I want him to feel confident about his body and to be able to walk with his head held high.'

Remember Mark, whom I mentioned at the beginning of this chapter? He isn't the Karate Kid type, but the only thing that we tried which worked to give him back his confidence was enrolment in the Quindo course. It gave him a positive body image and made him stop reacting like a victim. It also gave him self-confidence and self-esteem. (See Help Organisations.)

Here are a few things which might help your child:

- Find out about local classes in martial arts or confidence building.

- Find out what is happening locally that might be interesting and try to arrange to take your children.

- Check on the free days at museums and go with your children and friends. Make it a fun excursion and take your lunch and some treats for the children.

- Check on interactive children's theatres in your area.

- Enrol your child in a pottery class or tap dancing or cooking – check with your local authority.

- Find out about half price tickets for plays and support your local theatre groups.

- If your children have never been to a soccer or cricket match, take them and go.

- Watch out for specials from the railways when you can take your children on a day outing for a very small price or even free with your ticket.

- Get your children a library card and take them often to the library.

- Often there are concerts in parks or churches or libraries. Many children have never heard instruments played live. It might inspire them to learn an instrument.

- Find out about local clubs where your child can take part in sports or other activities.

- See if there is a scout or girl guide troop near you – if not, start one.

- Help out in a soup kitchen.

- Start your child out on a hobby, such as model building.

The more children try, the better the chance that they will find something they like and which will improve their self-esteem.

4. Find your child's strengths

'I just don't know what to do for my project,' Gareth, aged twelve, told his mother. Gareth's teacher had asked the class to write about what they saw themselves doing in ten years' time. 'Let's think about what you like to do and what you're good at and then see what kinds of things you could do with those strengths,' replied his mother. A wise woman, Gareth's mum. She was helping him to think for himself and to appreciate his own abilities.

O   Together they made a list of Gareth's strengths:

- Reading
- History
- Writing
- Thinking of ideas to save the environment
- Loving animals
- Playing rugby
- Good balance
- Good eyesight
- Gets along with friends
- Likes travelling
- Swimming
- Feeding the goldfish
- Good hand–eye co-ordination

When they had completed the list, they looked up a variety of jobs and activities in books in the library, knowing full well that in ten years' time there should be lots of other jobs not even thought of today. Gareth thought that being a vet was a great idea because he loves animals, but his lack of interest in science would probably be a hindrance. The idea of writing and broadcasting about environmental issues was very appealing, as was becoming a coach for sports because he enjoys sports and likes working with people. Being a travel guide was rejected because of Gareth's indifference to languages, but he thought he might write a travel guide.

Gareth eventually decided to do his project on being a broadcaster who played rugby with his local club on the weekends! He felt quite good about his project and learned that his strengths and interests now would probably influence what he did in later life.

If children can be helped to realise their own strengths, it can make a difference in their attitudes towards school, other children and themselves. Gareth's mother posted his strengths on the front of the refrigerator and noticed that Gareth would sometimes pause beside the fridge and read them over with a smile on his face.

O Help your children by:

- Making a list with them of their strengths

- Posting the list and updating it when necessary

- Encouraging them to think about their strengths

- Praising the things they do

- Finding examples of famous people who have used similar strengths to do exciting or interesting things in life

- Giving them biographies of people who have achieved things which you think your child might be interested in

- Encouraging them to ignore any weaknesses they can't change or which don't hinder them. Too often people focus on what they can't do rather than what they can do

5. Helping them to achieve

In the summer before the beginning of each new school year, Angela sits down with her children individually and helps them to think of what they would like to accomplish that year, academically, socially and in other areas. It isn't a great long list, but includes goals for the year and sometimes more long-term ones, like eventual career plans. One of Angela's daughters, Sophie, had been bullied at school the year before.

O   This is Sophie's list:

- ignore Natalie (school bully)
- tell if someone bullies me
- make friends with three girls
- get to school on time
- pay more attention in French
- turn in homework on time
- get to know at least one new student
- keep my old friends
- improve in gymnastics

Angela goes over the list with each of her children, listens to their concerns and makes suggestions. She also notes things that might signify a problem. Angela had been working with Sophie's teachers and hoped that the bullying was finally laid to rest, but she would be keeping an eagle eye to make sure that her daughter did not suffer any more. She was pleased to see that Sophie put on her list that she would tell if the bullying started up again, but even more pleased that Sophie was looking at other things besides the bullying. It indicated that Sophie was gaining back some self-confidence.

Put the list in a safe place and go over it once a term to see if the goals are being achieved and how you can help if they aren't.

O   Help your children to think about being successful by:

- getting them to think of what they want to achieve

- discussing with them how to reach their goals

- getting them to set realistic targets – being elected to Parliament at age eight might be a bit ambitious, but visiting Parliament and finding out how to go about becoming an MP is realistic

- helping them to break the goal into manageable bits (saving whales is a great idea, but perhaps it needs to be done in stages)

- updating their goals with them on a regular basis

6. Disappointment

Tom was desperate to get the lead part in the school play, but when the roles were announced, he was playing a minor character. He fled the school and came home, bursting into tears as he entered the door. His father knew how much he had practised and rehearsed for the audition and how much it meant to him. 'We all know that there are disappointments and discouraging things which happen in life. I've certainly had my fair share, but somehow it always seems worse if it happens to your child. You want to take the hurt away, take it on yourself instead of on your child.'

A completely understandable reaction – I feel the same way. But part of learning to have self-esteem inevitably includes setbacks. We can't always have what we want, neither can we let a failure to get something completely blow our self-confidence. If our children learn to deal with disappointments they will be less likely to be pulled down by depression and life's curve balls.

Tom's father didn't know what to say, so he engulfed his son in a big hug and told him soothingly that he was so proud that he had gone out for the play because he himself would never have had the courage to even try out. He didn't care what part he had, it was better than he had ever done as far as drama was concerned. To his delight his son stopped crying and looked at him in astonishment. His father was an executive with a large company and was always making presentations, so this was news to him.

What Tom didn't realise was that his father had always been terrified of getting up in front of people and had to screw up his courage even now. He also told Tom about the time when he was in school and had wanted to run for a student election. He practised and practised what he was going to say, but never went through with it – nerves got the better of him. But his father had taken a course in public speaking because he was determined to go into a business that demanded this skill. So even if he didn't enjoy it, he could do it.

Tom's father said he didn't know how to help him cope, but he instinctively did the right thing for Tom. By sharing his own sense of failure at not trying out for the student election, he showed him that people get through these things and are sometimes motivated to change things. He also made Tom feel good that he had been brave enough to go out for the play in the first place, something the father had been unable ever to do. Telling Tom he was proud of his achievement was like a balm to Tom.

○ To help children cope with disappointments:

- accept that it is important and don't say, 'It doesn't matter' – it obviously does matter to your child

- say you are sorry it happened

- give them hugs and attention, no matter how grown-up and big they are. Inside they feel about two and they want your support

- tell them about times when you were discouraged or disappointed, but try to mention how something good followed. No good saying something like, 'I never got over what happened.' WRONG! Choose your examples to help your child cope, not to encourage him or her to give up.

7. Be calm

'Ann is always wound up like a top,' complained her mother. 'If she is like this at her age, I hate to think of what will happen to her when she gets out into the real world.' Ann's mother is right to be concerned, but the funny thing is that she is ten times worse than her daughter, but doesn't know it! Guess where Ann has learned her behaviour from? No prizes for right answers – sorry!

I have a friend who drives us all to distraction. She never relaxes and wonders why we all make excuses to go after being with her for less than an hour. She cannot sit down and talk, and always finds something to do – make a fifth cup of coffee (maybe it's the caffeine?), plump up the cushions, fiddle with the cord of the telephone – it's perpetual motion. An hour in her company leaves me feeling slightly more hyper than the cartoon character 'The Road Runner'. The most noticeable problem she has, though, is that she is so busy being busy that she doesn't listen to anyone. She simply cannot relax long enough to engage in meaningful conversation. Sad, but true.

Back to Ann. Why do we care if our children relax or not? Because when you're relaxed you are receptive to other people, your mind is clearer and ready to accept information, your body isn't at war with itself and you can tune in to your own feelings and thoughts and, of course, you feel more self-confident.

Of course, there are times when you might function better if you are slightly tense and the adrenalin is flowing, perhaps before a big game or before a performance or test. But functioning on that level all the time just leads to burn-out and children need to know how to relax. Some of these techniques are also useful to help children stay calm if someone is trying to bully them.

○ You can help by:

• teaching them to sit or stand very still

• asking them to close their eyes and think of something calm, like a clear lake or a sunny meadow or a peaceful experience they have had (like sitting on Gran's lap and having a story read to them)

- teaching them to breathe deeply, slowly and calmly

- asking them to hold the thought that is relaxing them and to focus on it until they feel quite calm and still

- explaining that they can use this technique whenever they feel themselves getting upset or before they have to try to do something difficult or of great importance to them

The ability to relax helps children (and the rest of us) to put aside worries or distractions and to focus on what we need to do.

8. Encourage self-congratulation

I know, I know ... it's 'not done' to encourage self-congratulation. I can just hear you saying, 'We'll end up with precocious little monsters bragging about themselves – insufferable!' That isn't what I mean, actually, though I see nothing wrong with being able to say, 'I did that well.' No, what we're talking about is teaching children to *tell themselves* that they did well or that they can do a brilliant job. Ask your children to practise saying to themselves that they did a great job, and that they are going to succeed in their test (or whatever it is).

This is exactly the sort of thing top athletes and business people and actors and musicians do. They jig themselves up by saying, 'this is going to be my best performance ever' or

'I'm going to get that commission because I have the best product' or 'today I'm going to win that medal because I deserve it after all my hard work'. Sort of like – watch out world, here I come.

9. Self-talk

This is slightly different to self-congratulation. This is about those everyday thoughts children and young people have about themselves and what they say to themselves.

I don't know about you, but I do talk to myself. In fact in our office you might hear lots of self-talk as Jane tells herself what she is doing next and Lisa goes by saying aloud, 'Now, I've done that and have to ring so and so.' You would not survive in our office unless you talked to yourself. What has this to do with helping victims of bullying? I find that most victims of bullying talk to themselves and tell themselves 'I'm going to be bullied' or 'I don't have any friends' or 'I know I can't do that very well' or words to the effect that they are not in control or that they are not good people.

Suggest to your child that he or she start talking to themselves and saying positive things like 'I can cope' or 'I am strong' or 'I don't deserve to be treated like this'. Encourage them to put away negative old tapes that run round and round in their heads giving off bad messages. Tell them to shake their heads if the old bad messages start and to replace them with good messages. They can do this even if they don't at first believe the good messages. By listening to the old tapes, sometimes taken from what the bully has said to them, they become their own worst enemy.

You can ask your child to write down some positive messages or you can help him or her to do this. Ask them to practise (in private) saying aloud, 'I am a good person'. It sounds a little corny, but one of the most important things we can do with our children is to give them a positive voice inside which helps them to ward off things like bullying.

10. Strategies for repair

It is possible to help children who have lost their self-esteem through bullying. It certainly isn't easy and many of these ideas will take time and effort. Some will appeal more to some children than to others. All will take some acting and practice. Suggesting to children that they:

○   say thank you if anyone compliments them. A child with low self-esteem will reject compliments. This strategy is a good first step to helping these children to stop blocking out all the good things about themselves. Make an agreement with your child that he or she will just say a simple thank you from now on when anyone says something nice about them.

○   use humour. As you know I put humour at the top of my wish list for kids and everyone. This doesn't mean that a child should put up with bullying and make it a joke – it is never a joke. But a child who can make a witty retort like 'better red (read) than you' to a statement like 'Hey red' will deflect future bullying and shows that silly remarks aren't important.

○   lighten up. Do something silly. Have fun. Look for ways to be spontaneous. It is a good way to get rid of stress.

O   refuse to react. Walk away, look bored, look at the
     ceiling, ignore the whole situation. Tell themselves that
     they are too important to be bothered with this.

O   confront with attitude. If Mark could just make the
     intake-of-breath-through-teeth noise and shake his head
     with a slightly sarcastic look on his face like 'this is such
     a silly remark that it is beneath me to reply', the bullies
     would eventually have to find a new target. Again, this
     sort of thing takes practice and is best done in front of
     other kids to be appreciated.

O   think positively. 'No matter what they say, I'm a good
     person', 'I don't deserve to be picked on', 'I am great!', 'I
     can do it', 'I will do it'. Of course children may not
     actually feel this way at the time, but constant repetition
     does help. Tell children they are protecting their inner
     core – like a nuclear power station.

O   remember that the person or people bullying them are
     heading for trouble sooner or later (see chapter 3 on
     bullies). Tell them to think 'They can't destroy my life
     just because they are destroying their own.'

O   practise body posture. Stand tall, speak clearly, look
     confident even if you don't feel that way inside and act
     as if you are in charge of yourself.

O   throw back the insults using retorts like, 'I don't
     understand' or 'Pardon?' or 'Please explain yourself',
     all of which puts the onus on the bully to be more clever
     than he or she probably is.

O think 'water off a duck's back'. My father used to say that it was all 'water off a duck's back' whenever he was ignoring something. It creates a great word picture for your mind, thus giving you another protective coating like the nuclear power station above.

O distract. Distract yourself from what is happening. Think about a pleasant time and send your mind there. This helps you not to react.

O relax. Use the techniques mentioned above to calm yourself. The calmer you are the less chance there is for the slings and arrows to get through to you.

O be gentle to themselves. Don't be hard on yourself and beat yourself up for your mistakes. Everybody makes mistakes. Learn to laugh when you make a mistake. It isn't the end of the world!

O use their religious beliefs, if they have them. Meditating or praying can be very calming.

O remember that some very famous, successful people were bullied as kids and they've beaten the bullies by having wonderful, interesting lives:

- Winston Churchill
- Frank Bruno
- Phil Collins
- Duncan Goodhew
- Whitney Houston
- Jamie Lee Curtis
- Michele Pfeiffer

- Kevin Costner
- Sinead O'Connor
- Jean-Claude Van Damme
- Harrison Ford
- Sir Ranulph Fiennes

And many more I haven't named. If they can overcome it to go on to fame and fortune, so can you!

11. Make a plan

When you have sorted out with your child the things you both think he or she might be able to do to build self-confidence, make a plan. This plan can be written down or verbal. I find that writing something down gives it a bit more status, but that will depend upon the age and state of mind of your child. Whatever you do should not put more pressure on them. If a plan is agreed upon, it could look something like this:

MONDAY	Think one positive thought about myself
TUESDAY	Say one nice thing to someone at home
WEDNESDAY	Say one nice thing to someone at school
THURSDAY	Calm myself with deep breathing before going to the lunch room
FRIDAY	Find someone to walk home with

You see that this list is fairly non-threatening, but could be even less so if every day the task of your child was to say one good thing about themselves. That could go on for a week or two before moving up to talking to another child. Again, it has to depend upon the state your child is in and the co-operation you are getting from the school to stop the bullying.

12. Dos and don'ts for parents

Finally, a last few pointers for parents about the dos and don'ts of building self-esteem and self-confidence in our children:

O   DO

- Praise your child frequently. Make sure it isn't false praise or they won't buy it. Be specific. For example, tell a child that he is a genius when he isn't and your praise will be hollow. But say that you think he has done very well on a particular paper or in an event and it will be genuine and seen to be so by the child.

- Give lots of unconditional love. Say, 'I'm so glad you are my child', 'I love you', 'I like you'.

- Compliment your child's appearance by saying things like, 'I think you look pretty in that outfit', 'Green is a good colour on you', 'That shirt looks good on you'. Bullied children often think they are ugly or look strange, another problem of low self-esteem.

- Spend time with your child. If all the attention he or she is getting is negative, some positive attention from you every day will help.

- Play down your child's failures using phrases like, 'I know you're disappointed, but it will be better next time' or 'Just a bit of bad luck, don't worry'. Do say if the child needs to prepare more or plan better next time, but be sure to tell the child that this doesn't mean he is bad or worthless.

- Let your child make decisions and take responsibility. Self-esteem improves when children take some control over things in their lives.

- Make a list of all the positive things you can think of about your child. Show it to him.

- Set your child up to succeed. Try to arrange situations where your child will shine or do well.

○   DON'T

- Set unrealistic expectations for your child. More failure will only increase her misery.

- Continually criticise or put down your child. Her self-esteem is low enough without you adding to it.

- Be put off or hurt if your child rejects your praise and compliments. He may seem to reject it, but it is soothing his wounds.

- Give up. It takes a lot of time and patience to build or rebuild a child's self-esteem.

- Forget that a child needs a parent with good self-esteem.

If you haven't got it, use all the suggestions above, take out some books from the library and get to work on yourself.

If only children could take to heart the words of the writer Montaigne who lived in the sixteenth century: 'I care not so much what I am in the opinion of others as what I am in my own.' Indeed, if only we could all take that to heart, wouldn't life be grand?

POINTS TO REMEMBER

Children should try to remember that:

1. No one is perfect. You are only human and we all have doubts about ourselves from time to time and sometimes more often than that!

2. It is natural to make mistakes – that doesn't mean you are a bad person. Everyone makes mistakes. Forgive others their mistakes.

3. It is OK to try and fail. That is the way we learn.

4. Be kind to yourself. Don't beat yourself up.

5. You are a good person. There are lots of things you can do in life and do well.

6. No one is good at everything. Focus on your good points, not your bad ones.

7. Tell yourself 'I am a good person' at least five times a day.

8. Laugh at yourself. Have fun and enjoy life.

9. You can work things out — most problems are solvable.

10. Your parents think you are wonderful and they are there for you. Talk to them, confide in them and let them love you.

5

THE TRICK TO MAKING
FRIENDS

Eleven-year-old Terry was having an awful time at school. She had been bullied when she was younger, but that had now stopped. Terry's biggest problem was that she could not seem to make and keep friends. Some days everything seemed all right, but most days Terry would come home with tales of woe and feeling very unhappy.

In the mornings, Terry's mother would try to get her going to get to school on time, but the conversations generally went like this:

'I don't want to go to school. I don't have anyone to sit with at lunch or to play with during breaks. I don't have any friends.'

Terry's parents were distraught when then they came to me. 'She is so miserable that we don't know what to do. We can't find friends for her or make the other kids play with her. She's a great kid – clever and sweet. We just don't know why this is happening.'

Obviously they didn't want to do the wrong thing and they loved their daughter very much. In fact, Terry's family was wonderful. They did lots of things together, played games, had family meals, helped their children with their school work and they seemed to all get on in a really positive way.

I think that Terry's problems stem from the time she was

bullied. She had lost her confidence in herself to make and keep friends. I worked with her parents and some of the things we tried are listed later in this chapter. There is no foolproof way to help children make friends, but some things do seem to work. More on that later.

Not having friends is very difficult for children. You can imagine the lonely feelings when you have no one to sit with at lunch or play with in the playground or go to visit after school. Yet some children never seem to lack for friends. They seem to be able to naturally attract people and are full of confidence. Are there some things we can teach children about finding friends and being a friend to others? You bet there are and some are very simple. The earlier we start the better. But there is one caution – some children will be very happy having one or two friends or a small group, while others like being friends with everyone.

Even in the same family children will differ in how they perceive friendship. Andrew, aged nine, loves being in the midst of a shouting, rowdy, tumbling group of children. As far as he is concerned the more the merrier, and he isn't happy unless there is action most of the time. His brother Brandon, aged fifteen, has always had a few close friends and likes to get together to talk or go to the cinema or play a game of chess or just go for walks in the woods. Their father can't understand how they could be so different, but they are both content so there is no need to try to change things. If it isn't broken, don't fix it.

But if you do need to 'fix it', here are some tips about making friends which you can try with your children:

1. FIND OUT WHAT IS HAPPENING

Did Terry have friends at one time or has she always been a loner? Has there been a 'growing apart' between a group of kids leaving her out in the cold? It turned out that Terry was a bright girl who seemed to have one or two friends at a time. One of her friends, Laura, had turned against her when the other children were bullying her. This had been a big blow for Terry, who had never been disloyal to people. She felt betrayed and hurt. Marilyn, her other friend, seemed to be moving on to form new friendships, something Terry felt unable to do. Terry was a slightly introverted child and her previous friendships had come largely through the efforts the other children made to get to know her. She didn't approach them, but was delighted to be approached and included in things. She had no family, behaviour or academic problems, but the bullying had left her slightly unsure of herself and convinced at one level that other children would not like her.

A discussion with Terry brought out some of her worries. Because she had never had to make the first move to find friends, the very idea of trying to go up to a 'new' person or group terrified her. She simply did not know how to begin or even who she might like to be friends with now. She also felt rejected by Marilyn who was spending less and less time with her because of the new friends she was making. Terry had put all her eggs (her two friendships) in one basket and now the basket was empty.

For some children there will be other problems, such as a personal habit which turns people off, like wiping their nose on their sleeve, or terrible family problems which make it difficult for the child to think about anything else, including

103

making friends, or they may live a long way from the rest of the class and miss out on socialising with the others after school or on weekends, or they may be picking on children themselves. It always pays to find out as much information as possible about the problem before you can begin to solve it.

2. DECIDE ON A PLAN

I asked Terry if I could help her make a list of children she might like to know. The list included Marilyn and four other girls. We figured out a plan that Terry felt she could do. One of the girls on her list, Gill, seemed quite nice, but also a bit shy. This was an ideal person for Terry to try to approach because Gill would probably welcome someone attempting to get to know her. The plan was:

○ that Terry and her parents would sit down together and figure out what Terry likes in a friend and what friends might like from her.

○ for her parents to talk with the teacher to ensure that everything possible was being done to include Terry with the other children and to find out if there were any problems we didn't know about.

○ for Terry to roleplay with me to give her the confidence she felt she needed to seek out friends. I pretended to be the child that Terry was going to approach and Terry tried out a few ideas with me (see Roleplay below). We worked on:

- eye contact. Looking in a pleasant way at people shows you are interested in them.

- listening to what the other person says. Children need to be told that listening is an important skill. Everyone likes for other people to pay attention to what they say – it makes them feel good.

- looking friendly. No one wants to be around someone who glowers and emits unfriendly signals. Sometimes unhappy children need to act friendly, even if they don't feel that way.

- opening lines when approaching another child. 'I really like this game, may I please join in?'

○ to invite Gill over to do something specific like going to the cinema or riding bikes or going to the park.

If you are forming a plan with your child, it might not include all these steps, depending upon the circumstance. It may be that your child is new to a school and doesn't know anyone yet, but feels uncomfortable about making new friends. In that case you might just help by letting your child practise on you what to say or by getting advice from the teacher. Inviting children over might be all that needs to happen.

3. GET HELP AT SCHOOL

Most friendships are formed in school, so it is vital to get the teacher's help. Perhaps the seating arrangements could be

changed to encourage more friendships forming. In Terry's class, the teacher had allowed the children to choose who they sat next to every day. After being alerted by Terry's parents, he decided to assign seats and change the seating plan every three weeks. This gave children a chance to get to know more people and it helped develop new friendships. It certainly helped Terry, as the teacher made sure that she was at a table with Gill, which gave the girls an opportunity to get to know each other.

You can also ask that the lunch-room and playground situations be discreetly monitored so that conflicts or hurtful incidents can be stopped before they get out of hand. It is best if this is all done with the knowledge of your child, but if this is not possible, you should contact the teacher in confidence for the good of your child. Most teachers are only too pleased to help.

If you get no co-operation or feel that the teacher might make it worse, which unfortunately does sometimes happen, then see if there is someone else at the school with whom you could have a quiet word to enlist their help. Often the playground supervisors or lunch-room staff (called 'dinner ladies' in my day!) are people from your neighbourhood and they might be able to at least let you know what is going on with your child from their viewpoint. Also they might be able to intervene in unassuming ways because they know the kids and their parents. In my school, the dinner ladies remembered when my dad was there. I was gobsmacked, as they say. Then it seemed impossible that anyone could be that old and still working. Now they seem young!

4. TALK ABOUT FRIENDSHIP

Many studies have been done to find out what qualities people look for in a friend and what makes a good friend. I conducted a survey of 200 seven- to eleven-year-olds in a school close to where I live and asked them what they looked for in a friend. I also asked teachers to set out their observation about why they thought some children were more 'popular' than others. Here's what both groups said:

- When children are looking for friends they are drawn to someone who:

    1) smiles and is happy most of the time
    2) likes to join in things and plays with them
    3) isn't bossy
    4) helps them with their school work
    5) shares things
    6) makes them laugh and is fun to be with
    7) listens when they want to talk
    8) is kind
    9) sticks up for them
    10) doesn't change – they aren't nice one day and mean the next

- Teachers observed that children who were 'popular' with both students and teachers:

    1) were self-confident
    2) were good at organising games and activities
    3) could shrug off disappointment and setbacks
    4) were good listeners
    5) had a good sense of humour

6) had parents who were supportive
7) had good communication skills, including being able to find something to talk about with other children and adults
8) were healthy and often good at sports
9) were able to sort out conflicts between children
10) complimented others and were not critical

It might be a good idea to either duplicate this list and discuss it with your children or make up a list of your own with them. Better yet, let them make one up themselves and then you discuss it with them. It is an excellent exercise that gets children thinking about not only what they want in a friend, but how they are acting with other children. You might suggest to your child's teacher that, if time can be found, they may want to try a similar exercise with the class.

I found it very useful when I was teaching to get the children talking about friendship because it prevented problems forming. It was much more positive for the children to say to someone, 'You're not being very kind' instead of 'I hate you, go away'. At least the child knows what to try to correct or talk about rather than wondering exactly why he or she has suddenly become hated. The word 'hate' was banned from my classroom and the children learned to be more constructive. That isn't to say that they were all friends, all the time. It wasn't Utopia, but it was fairly amicable.

Terry and her parents came up with a list that looked like this:

● What Terry wanted in a friend was someone who:

1) would be nice to her and not bully her
2) enjoyed talking, music, games, making up plays

3) would be her friend at lunch and playtime
4) would like to come over to her house
5) was kind and thoughtful
6) was not too loud or boisterous
7) liked to laugh

- What Terry thinks a friend might want from her was:

1) loyalty
2) to do things together outside of school
3) to sit with her at lunch and be together at breaks
4) to trust her
5) to organise things to do
6) to be trusted with secrets
7) to stand up for her if she was bullied

When we met, Terry thought she was a nice person, but perhaps a bit too sensitive because of the bullying. She looked for slights when they weren't happening. In other words, if someone didn't invite her to play, she felt rejected. We talked about how the other children just went up and joined in games, but she felt too unsure to do that just yet. I asked her to observe how the children got involved and to see if she could try to follow their lead.

Terry also began thinking of things she and friends could do, like go roller skating or to the park to play. Her parents were more than willing to provide opportunities for Terry and her friends to do some fun things, as long as they didn't cost much money.

Terry also thought she had to work on a way to actually go up to Gill and start a conversation. She tended to get tongue-tied, so we decided to practise – just the two of us so she wouldn't be embarrassed.

5. ROLEPLAY

Starting a conversation with someone or going up to a group to talk can be daunting. Adults I know who find it difficult say that any intelligent thought they've ever had vanishes and they become blithering idiots. That sounds a bit harsh and self-critical, but if that's how they feel it's no wonder they hold back. What children need is a practised phrase or two they can use that slips out easily and gets them over that first hurdle. Terry and I came up with the following ideas for opening sentences:

- 'Did you see the programme last night about . . . ? What did you think of it?' Since many children watch television, this could be a common starting point.

- 'What did you think about the story we had to read for homework (or in class)?'

- 'I liked your drawing. What kinds of things do you like to draw?'

- 'What did you do over the holidays (or weekend)?'

- 'Would you like to go over there and play that game or do you have any other suggestions?'

- 'Would it be OK if I sat here next to you?'

We practised with Terry being herself and me being the various children such as Marilyn and Gill. I know Terry felt silly at first, but her confidence increased tremendously and she was able to try it out with the children. She was thrilled to tell me at our next meeting that it worked and children actually talked to her and sat with her at lunch. Parents may feel awkward doing roleplay but it is worth overcoming this for the sake of your child.

If children are old enough, explain the difference between a 'closed' question and an 'open' question. A closed question is more likely to elicit a plain yes or no response. 'Do you like cheese?' 'Yes.' These kinds of questions usually start with words like do, did, is, are, was.

Open questions, starting with how, what, when, why, are more likely to elicit a longer response with more opportunities for conversation. 'What sort of things did you do this summer?' 'Oh, we went swimming and I read some good books. I tried playing tennis a little bit, but I'm not very good at it.'

There is no guarantee that the person you are talking with will give you a better answer with an open question, but at least you are setting up the odds more in your favour.

6. INVITE CHILDREN OVER

In order to cement friendships and foster new ones, it often helps to have your children play at your home with others. This not only gives them the chance to get to know each other away from school, but gives you a chance to observe how your children are interacting and what their friends are like.

Try to make sure that a fun time is had by the children. Help your child to think of fun things to do such as arranging a trip to the cinema or going to the park with a picnic. Maybe there is a swimming baths near you or an ice rink. It is also fun to do things the children might not do at home. I remember teaching a group of my son's friends how to play monopoly and some card games. They had never done that before, which amazed me. I guess computer games have taken over the world when I wasn't looking!

Terry invited Gill over and they went to the cinema and took Terry's dog for a walk in the park. Both girls had a good time. Terry now plans to ask Marilyn and the other girls to go ice skating and back to her house for a pizza.

7. WATCH WHAT IS HAPPENING

If you can unobtrusively observe your children when they are with friends or trying to make friends, you can find out lots that might help. Obviously you can't be in the room the whole time your child is playing with friends, but you can be 'reading' next door or rearranging pictures in the hallway nearby or weeding the garden while they are outside. Leave the door ajar so you can overhear what's happening or set up a game or tea in the kitchen and busy yourself in the background. Observe if your child is being friendly, judgemental, bossy, shy, too sensitive, tactful, humorous, aggressive or complaining.

Then try to encourage the traits mentioned previously that enhance friendships and to gently suggest ways to change the others (one at a time, please). If your child is being too sensitive, you might gently suggest that sometimes people misunderstand what others are saying because they take things too seriously. Explain that reacting by crying or going into a shell doesn't help because it makes others withdraw. Help your child to see that the other person did not mean to hurt her feelings and that she should not take things to heart so much. If your child is too bossy, tell her not to be! Most likely she got it from you. Seriously, bossiness puts kids right off and we need to help our children to share and not to feel that they can make all the decisions.

Terry's parents said that she was very kind and caring when they saw her with Gill. She made sure that Gill had fun, let Gill play with her things and allowed Gill to choose the film they saw. But they also observed that Terry was hypersensitive. Fortunately, Gill didn't seem bothered. Now Terry's parents are working with her to get her to try to laugh things off more. One of the most common things I see in families where children are having difficulty making friends and where children have been bullied, is the family itself seems to be rather sensitive. Not all families are like this, but if yours is, try to work on not taking everything to heart. And if you are too sensitive, tell your child and explain why this can sometimes be counter-productive because you spend too much time worrying about little things that don't really matter. Children like to know that we have to struggle with the same problems they do. It gives them hope.

I honestly think that if I could tell parents of newborn babies one thing to do with their children after loving them, it would be to laugh a lot and help them develop a sense of humour.

8. CHANGE BEHAVIOUR

In Terry's case there was no undesirable behaviour to change, unless you count her sensitivity. I wouldn't call that bad behaviour – more a sense of perspective. However, there are some children who don't have friends because they turn people off.

If children are aggressive, have a quick temper, are bossy or refuse to share, other children will not want to play with them. If they have nasty habits like farting, burping, picking their noses or spitting, they will find everyone taking a wide berth. If they have poor personal hygiene such as body odour or greasy hair, then it is not surprising they lack friends.

It is possible to change children's behaviour or personal hygiene if they, and their parents, are willing to try. I remember one boy who was so smelly that no one could bear to be around him. When I gently and, I thought, tactfully tried to talk with his mother about it, I was told it was none of my business and the family, which seemed normal in other respects, didn't believe in washing much because it was harmful to the body. Oh dear. The trouble is the boy knew he smelled and hated it.

I'm afraid I circumvented the mother on this one. We arranged for him to shower at school and put on fresh clothes we kept for him. So every day he would come in the clothes from home, wash, change, spend the day in his 'school clothes' (several different outfits) and then change back into his 'home clothes' and go home. Mother never did find out and the boy went on to become a very clean carpenter.

If children are acting in a way which clearly needs to be changed for their own good and for the good of others, don't hesitate to wade in. Practise alternative ways to behave until they become second nature. Arrange a time-out place for the child to go when he or she is feeling aggressive so they won't bother someone else. Tell them if they are bossy and explain how to approach people in a nice way — roleplay with them *asking* kids to do things instead of *telling* everyone what to do. Don't look the other way if a child is picking his or her nose. Confront yucky habits, tell the child this is unacceptable in polite society and reward them when they don't do it. It isn't cute to be obnoxious.

9. IT DOESN'T ALWAYS WORK OUT

Friendships won't always go according to plan. A child may try to be friends with someone, but it just doesn't work out for reasons beyond control. It could just be that they really can't find anything in common. It might be that the children were friends but now enjoy doing completely different things. Or a friend may have personal problems and just want to be left alone for a while.

Friends also may decide to do something which your child cannot or will not do, like steal or joy ride. At least we all hope our children would draw the line at that kind of destructive friendship. One thing we need to emphasise to our children is that friends do not force people to do things that are harmful to themselves or to others. So if a friend says 'let's steal from the store and if you don't I'm not your friend any more' or 'if you don't join in bullying that kid, then our friendship is over', the friendship wasn't 'worth spit' as a five-year-old once said to me! Couldn't say it better myself.

The important message to get across to your children is that some friendships do come and go. Some will last a lifetime, others only a day. If they have tried their best, perhaps it just wasn't meant to be, as my grandmother used to say. Talk with them about friendships that fail, if they want to talk, and assure them that there are lots of people out there to become friends with so don't despair. It does help if you can talk about a time when you lost a friend and what it meant to you. After all, your children can see that you've survived it and that is a good role-model for them.

10. DEVELOP NEW SKILLS, ACTIVITIES, INTERESTS

Finally, help your children increase the number of people they can be friends with by encouraging them to develop their skills and interests. If a child is good at sports, find out about Saturday sports clubs or after-school lessons. Look into swimming, dance, tennis and gymnastics classes. Check out the local Scout troops, Brownie packs, acting or martial arts classes. See if you can arrange group music lessons. Not only will these things increase your children's self-confidence, they will give them a whole new group of people from which to find friends.

And whatever you do, please encourage your children not to discard old friends as they make new ones. Fickle friends break many a heart, as Terry found out with Laura. Most of the best friends I have are those I have known for over thirty years, some are school friends. Perhaps that's because they haven't been around me much! Still, I think we can take a leaf out of the book of a fifteenth-century writer, John Seldon, who said: 'Old friends are best. King James used to call for his old shoes; they were the easiest on his feet.'

POINTS TO REMEMBER

If your children need some tips about making and keeping friends, suggest that they:

1. smile, be pleasant and say hello to people. We are all more attracted to nice people.

2. make the first move. Reach out to other children and don't always wait for someone else to say hello or ask you to do something.

3. learn to be a good listener. Everyone likes to be listened to and it is one of the things children value most in a friend. Explain to your children that they should look at people while they are talking and concentrate on what they are saying.

4. don't expect everyone to be just like them. It is better to have friends who have their own ideas and opinions than ones who are all exactly alike. Point out that it would be boring if we all thought and acted the same.

5. ask lots of questions. A good way to let other people know you are interested in them is to ask about what they like and what they think.

6. don't moan all the time. If you only use your friends to talk about your problems, they will get tired of hearing constant tales of woe. Talk about good things as well.

7. beware of false friends. Sometimes we stay with friends because there is no one else around. Watch out for 'friends' who try to get them to do things they don't want to do or which they know are wrong.

8. don't be bossy or show off all the time. It gets really boring if someone always wants to be in charge or is always bragging about how great they are.

9. try to think of things to do which might be interesting. It is fun to be around people who are creative and have good ideas.

10. don't bug people – if they don't want to be friends, move on to someone else. Not all friendships work out.

6

WORKING WITH THE SCHOOL

Valerie, aged fourteen, waited until the last week of term to tell her mother about the bullying which had gone on for most of the year. For some reason which Valerie could not figure out, she had been the target of a group of sixteen-year-old girls. These girls had followed her, written things about her on the chalk board, made hurtful comments and made her life absolutely miserable.

Valerie was a very pretty girl, intelligent and hard working. She had never encountered bullying before and was shocked and surprised that she was the target of so much hatred. It did not surprise me that the bullies were marginal students, but it did surprise me that they were popular, pretty girls themselves. These young people had no need to be jealous of Valerie or to embark on this bullying campaign. It turned out that one of the girls, Alice, thought Valerie was after her boyfriend (untrue) and that was the start of the whole mess. Instead of finding out the facts, Alice decided to attack Valerie and to get her friends to join in. Such was Alice's clout with the students, that no one questioned her when she announced that Valerie had been spreading rumours and 'needed sorting out'.

The only reason Valerie finally told about the bullying was because she felt safe – these girls were leaving school at the end of term and Valerie had held up as long as she could.

What upset Valerie's mother the most was that it seemed no one at school realised that this gang was bullying her daughter. How could that be?

To be fair to the school, in this case the girls had been terribly clever and managed to pull off their stunts when there was no staff around. And Valerie had not told anyone except her best friend and Valerie had sworn her to secrecy. Without this friend I think Valerie would have cracked under the strain. As it was, she continued to do well in most of her subjects and hide the pain she was in.

When Valerie's mother said she would go and see the teacher, Valerie cried and pleaded with her not to go.

This is not unusual. Your child may beg you not to talk to the teachers and this will place you in a difficult position. If the bullying is happening at school, then the school needs to do something about it. You can certainly try to work it out with your child alone, if that is what you both think is best, but rarely does that solve the problem. Try to talk with your child about who they think would be the best person to deal with the problem at school and then work out a plan together. Whatever you do, don't ignore the bullying as it will most likely only get worse or even lead to your child trying something desperate to get away from it.

Valerie's mother thought she should let the school know that the bullying had gone on, even if the bullies were leaving the school. After all, there may be other victims and why should these girls be allowed to get away with their atrocious behaviour? Valerie argued that she would not have told her mother if she thought her mother would go to the school. After several days of debate and heated discussions, they compromised. Valerie's mother would talk to a teacher Valerie liked, but only after the girls had left the school.

Personally I felt the school should have been told and the

girls pulled up short for the way they had behaved. They left that school knowing they had hoodwinked everyone and got away with murder. It cannot be good for their characters that they succeeded in bullying. I imagine they have gone on to treat people they work with in the same way they treated Valerie. Also the school was not given a chance to show what they would do.

It is true that some schools, even when staff are told about bullying, do nothing or make light of it as the headteacher did in the case of Katherine mentioned in the first chapter of this book. It is unforgivable when staff take no action to stop bullying when they find out it is happening. In that case you may have to remove your child from the school, but we are getting ahead of ourselves here. Let's start with contacting the school.

CONTACTING THE SCHOOL

If you are going to approach the school, try to get your child to agree with your actions. If that is not possible and the bullying continues, try these steps:

1. Ring and make an appointment with the teacher – don't just show up, especially if you are angry, as it will start things off on the wrong foot and it is unlikely that the teacher will be able to see you anyway because of teaching schedules. Also most schools ask for parents to make appointments. If it is urgent, say so, and ask for a meeting as soon as possible and certainly within a day or two. If your child is upset to an alarming degree then

keep the child with you until you sort things out at school. Otherwise, make sure that your child is safe and feels safe going to school.

2. Try not to overreact, even if you are rightly furious. This could frighten your child into silence or even prompt him or her to retract.

3. Sit and write down everything you can about the bullying that has happened so far. Make sure that you put in as many times, dates and names as you can find out. This helps when you are making your case with the school.

4. Bring this written record of what has happened with you to the meeting, as well as copies of any letters you may have written and details of any telephone calls. This makes it easier to remember and to check on facts, if necessary. Keep a note of everyone you speak to about the bullying and keep copies of any correspondence.

5. Listen to the teacher's explanation and say that you want to work together with them to stop the bullying. It is always better if there is co-operation between the parents and the school.

6. If you feel unsure about the meeting or if there has been any antagonism between you and the school, bring along someone else to the meeting who could be a witness to what is said.

7. Make out a short list of points you want to cover in the meeting and use it as a reminder.

8. Ask to see a copy of the school's anti-bullying policy.

9. If the problem has not got out of hand yet, ask that the children work together on a solution. This is a particularly good approach if your child has been part of a group, which has somehow come unstuck. When this happens, the children usually have some residue of good feelings which can be used to resolve the bullying. The best outcome from your child's view may be that his old friends and he make up or that they are at least sympathetic and stop bullying.

10. If the problem is one of sustained bullying from someone or a group which has no previous friendship with your child and it cannot be resolved as above, then find out what the school is going to do about it. They should:

    ● ensure that your child is safe
    ● investigate what has happened
    ● interview the victim and bully separately
    ● interview witnesses
    ● depending upon the situation, they should take appropriate action such as:

        * obtain an apology
        * inform the bully's parents
        * insist that anything which was taken or destroyed be returned or replaced
        * provide support for the victim and a safe place, if necessary
        * ensure that the bullying stops by supervising the bully

* giving the bully help to change his or her behaviour
* let you know what is happening

Set a mutually agreed time limit for the action to take place.

11.   If you feel that the bullying has not stopped and nothing you agreed is being done, then make an appointment with the headteacher. Ask how cases of bullying are handled in the school. Explain that you really want to co-operate to end the problem but that you have so far been getting nowhere and your child is suffering.

IF BULLYING DOES NOT STOP

If the bullying goes on, do not just accept the situation. It may be that you have to take your child out of school because he or she is subject to continued attack and harassment.

1.   If necessary take your child to your GP and get a written excuse to keep him or her away from school due to the stress of bullying. Sometimes a brief break can give the child the fortitude to carry on. Be aware that there is controversy about this. Most teachers will advise you to send your child to school and even compare it to riding a horse and being thrown – get back on and keep riding. The message is the more time you take off, the more difficult it will be to go back to school. Yes, but how difficult is it for a child to go into a hellish bullying situation every day and why should they have to? If the

school can guarantee your child's safety and well-being, that's one thing. If they can't, I think you should keep your child at home.

2. Try to find out if there is a bigger problem in the school with bullying than just the one with your child. Contact other parents and ask. It may be that the school has always swept the problem under the carpet by stalling or ignoring parental concerns. If there are other cases, form an action group and proceed together.

3. Contact the Board of Governors. Your school has the names and addresses or will pass the letter or request on for you.

4. If the Governors don't help, then contact the Local Education Authority. Complain in writing to the Director of Education. Begin your letter with, 'I am writing to make a formal complaint . . .'

5. You can also write to the Secretary of State for Education. If your child is in a Grant Maintained School, you may use the following wording when writing:

    'I am writing to complain and ask you to use your powers under Sections 496 and/or 497 of the Education Act 1996 because I believe that the school is acting unreasonably.' Then as concisely as possible set out your case.

6. If the matter is not dealt with, contact your County Councillor or local MP. Make an appointment to see them at their surgery. Ask them to speed things up for you. If

you have written to the Secretary of State for Education, ask the MP for help in getting a reply.

7. Don't be fobbed off with empty promises to 'look into things'. Ask for specific action. 'I want the bullying of my child to be stopped immediately. I expect that he or she will be safe in school and able to learn, free from intimidation and harassment.'

8. Contact the police (see chapter 10) if the bullying is serious or sustained.

9. If you are really getting nowhere, see if you can interest a local journalist in your story. You might want to let the school know that you have reached the end of your tether and that the press will be contacting them. It might be that they do not want the bad publicity and that action is suddenly taken! But also be prepared for a possible backlash from the bullies and their supporters. You will need to ensure that your child is safe.

Schools have a duty of care towards their pupils. The school is *in loco parentis* and must provide an adequate and efficient education. If your child's education is being disrupted by bullying, you have the right to say that you believe the school is failing in its 'duty of care'.

LAST RESORT

If you feel that no one is helping and that the situation with the school has become impossible:

1. Get a sick note from the doctor if your child is really stressed and keep him or her home until you can make other arrangements.

2. Remove your child from that school, and find another which has a strong policy against bullying. In some cases I have dealt with, the child who was the victim of bullying in one school thrives and has no problems in the new 'anti-bullying' school. One can only conclude that it wasn't the child who had the problem, but the school which allowed it to go on.

3. Educate your child at home with the help of organisations like Education Otherwise. The law says you must educate your child, it does not say it has to be done in a school setting. (See chapter 11, Home Education.)

Most bullying situations will never reach these later steps. It seems that most schools now want to deal with bullying, but you may be unlucky.

If schools do not deal with the problem of bullying, then parents should suggest to schools that they take on the following suggestions:

CRACK THE CODE OF SILENCE

Suggest that the headteacher or teacher contact KIDSCAPE and ask for all of our information on stopping bullying in schools. KIDSCAPE will even send them a copy of an anti-bullying policy they can use as a model to set up their own. In the cases where both a parent and the school have contacted KIDSCAPE, there has been remarkable progress to stop bullying in the school.

To crack the code of silence, KIDSCAPE encourages the schools to:

1. become 'telling' schools. The headteacher makes it clear that bullying is unacceptable. Bullies will not be tolerated. The children have an obligation to *tell* if they are bullied or see bullying take place.

2. ensure that the adults do something when they are told. Adults have an obligation to *act*. For this approach to work, children must be able to rely on a sympathetic and helpful response if they do tell. In this way they learn that speaking out will make things better; keeping quiet will make things worse. Experience has shown that bullying is much less likely to happen in schools with a clear policy against bullying.

SET UP STUDENT HELPERS

The idea of using students to help others is as old as teaching itself. I used this method over twenty-five years ago when I had a classroom of thirty-four children and a few older children were making it their business to bully the younger ones:

1. At the start of the school year, assign new students an older 'helper' who acts as an adviser, protector and

mentor. Usually older or bigger children pick on younger or smaller ones, *who are alone*. This eliminated that problem and the older children took pride in helping 'their' charges. Of course you had to prepare the older children and instill in them a sense of responsibility, but that wasn't difficult. If a helper was a problem, we didn't allow him or her to be in the programme. The competition to be good enough to be a helper was immense and quite a positive force in the school.

2. We also set up student counsellors who were chosen anonymously by the children and teachers as 'people you would most likely seek out to talk to about a problem'. They were the natural helpers in the school. We gave them some extra training and they became the liaisons for children who felt they needed more than their regular helpers because of a particular bullying problem. We made sure the student counsellors had a place and a time to talk with the children and privacy to do so. It was a bit of extra time and trouble for all of us, but the results were excellent. Some schools are still using the student counsellors with great success.

SET UP 'BULLY COURTS'

As with the suggestion about setting up student helpers, I have always found that one of the most effective deterrents to bullying is other kids. In other words, if bullies can be made to feel that their behaviour is unacceptable *to the other children*, they will be much more likely to change than if they are simply told by adults to mend their ways. To bring this form of change about, KIDSCAPE advocates:

1. setting up 'bully courts', in which bully and victim are brought together, with a teacher and perhaps the parents, to discuss the causes and effects of what has happened.

2. ensuring that the 'courts' are part of a whole school policy within a school atmosphere in which bullying is stripped of any glamour and clearly condemned as wrong. These 'court' collaborations can change a bully's behaviour and make the children feel they have a direct involvement in stopping bullying.

TEACHER OR STAFF MEMBER IS THE BULLY?

Some of the most difficult cases we have had to deal with at KIDSCAPE have been when a teacher or a member of staff is reported to be bullying children by picking on them, humiliating them or taunting them. If you discover that your child is being bullied in this way:

1. You should talk with the teacher, if possible, and express your concerns. Perhaps your child has misinterpreted something that was said or done and it can be straightened out without a fuss.

2. However, if you feel the situation is beyond this kind of repair and that you cannot speak to the teacher or member

of staff, then see the headteacher and explain what has happened. In some schools you have to go through the head to make an appointment to see teachers anyway.

3. Keep a written record of the incidents and how they have affected your child. It may be that the teacher is unaware of what he or she is doing and that the bullying will stop. Or it may be that the teacher's way of dealing with children is not suited to your child (or any child) and the teacher needs to be talked with and shown more positive ways of interacting. Whatever the reasons, if the teacher is bullying children, then it should be stopped immediately.

4. If possible find out if other children are or have been bullied by this person. Get statements and ask them to support you.

5. If the bullying goes on, then get in contact with the Governors and follow the steps laid down above. At all stages, keep written records and, if you can see that it is necessary, bring along someone as an independent witness to meetings.

6. If ultimately it doesn't stop and all avenues fail, then find another school. A school that would condone bullying by anyone, especially a member of staff, is not a fit place to be in charge of children. I bet that member of staff was one of those little bullies who was never challenged and just grew up to be a big bully.

It is important to emphasise that there is a positive note when talking about dealing with schools. It is becoming more and more common for schools to take bullying very seriously and deal with it effectively. If you are unlucky enough to have your child enrolled in one of the ineffective and bad schools, try everything but ultimately you will probably have to look for one of those good schools. When you do look, ask the headteacher:

1. for a copy of the school's anti-bullying policy. It should be readily available and very clear.

2. what they do if they find a child is being bullied.

3. if you can observe the interaction of the children on the playground and at lunch. Note the level of supervision.

4. if you can talk to another parent of a child the same age as yours.

5. if your child can visit and if the headteacher will arrange for another child to either take your child around or to talk to. This can be a big comfort for children.

Observe for yourself how the staff interacts when you see them. Do they greet one another and seem content? Are the children well behaved and do they seem to be enjoying themselves as well as being nice to each other? Of course it is unrealistic to think that you will get a full measure of the school in a brief visit, but find out as much as possible before you find that you have transferred your child out of the frying pan and into the fire. In general, an open, welcoming headteacher who is willing to admit that bullying does happen but that they take it seriously and stop it, is a good indication that this new school is where you want your child.

RELUCTANT TO MOVE

Some children will tell you that they want to stay at their old school even if they have been and are being badly bullied. This happens because the child has either developed a victim mentality or because they feel 'better the devil you know'. This is not unusual. We often find that abused children will cling to and love the parent who is abusing them because at least they know the situation and it is better than the unknown. Some people choose to stay in terrible jobs for the same reason.

For the bullied child, he or she knows who the bullies are and they are probably afraid that it might be worse somewhere else. Sometimes you as the parent must make the decision for the child or encourage the child to leave if you know that the school is not going to protect your child. Do keep in mind that your child may have some friends at school that he or she doesn't want to leave so the final decision must take into account many factors.

If you want more advice on contacting schools or you just want to talk it through before you go in, give the KIDSCAPE Bullying Counsellor a ring. The times and telephone number are listed in the Help Section.

POINTS TO REMEMBER

When you find out your child has been bullied or that your child is a bully, the first point of contact will probably be the school. Keep in mind that:

1. most schools want to nip bullying in the bud and will try to co-operate with you.

2. talk to your child to find out how he or she perceives the situation.

3. you need to have as many facts as possible before contacting the school. Write down everything that you can find out.

4. it is possible that your child has the 'wrong end of the stick' and things are not as they seem.

5. a calm approach should accomplish greater co-operation than a screaming match.

6. you should not be fobbed off with empty promises. You want to know what steps will be taken and when.

7. schools have a duty of care to your child and are acting *in loco parentis*.

8. if the school is disorganised or poorly led or has bullying staff, you are in for a fight. Get help,

contact other parents, follow the procedures laid out in this chapter.

9.   some schools will try to make out that your child, a victim of bullying, has problems and needs help when, if the bullying were stopped, your child would be fine. Don't accept 'blame the victim'.

10.   your child's education and safety are the top priority. Don't use your child to get at and try to change a school that won't deal with bullying. It isn't fair to your child. There are times when it is best to cut and run and get your child into a decent school.

7

BULLYING THE BABIES

Four-year-old Helen started nursery school with great excitement. She could hardly wait to get to 'her school' every morning. But then her mother noticed a dramatic change. Helen started finding excuses not to go and asked her mother if she could stay home and help instead of going to school. When Helen's mother asked the staff if they thought something was the matter, she was assured that Helen was fine.

Helen was not fine. Another child, Edward, was constantly picking on Helen whenever he could get away with it. He was careful not to bully her when anyone was watching. The bullying was found out only when Helen burst into tears and told her mother.

It seems that cases of very young children being bullied are becoming more frequent. KIDSCAPE runs a helpline for parents and in the past couple of years we have had a tremendous increase in the number of calls from distressed parents of under-fives. Their children are coming home from nursery, reception and first-year classes with bruises, torn clothes and woeful tales of being called names and bullied. When the parents complain to the school, they may be told that this is just part of human nature, something children must learn to cope with if they are to survive the rough-and-tumble of everyday life.

This is completely the wrong attitude. It might be true that some little ones find the playground jungle a foreign place at first, so some think that any distress shown by young children is just natural. Initially a child may find it all a bit much, but parents need to know that bullying can and does go on even at this early age. Some teachers may say that bullying doesn't affect children and isn't important. One said 'it was only children playing – it wasn't bullying'. The teacher was responding to a parent's concern that her child was being consistently punched and pushed by another child.

It turned out that the punching child, Amy, was lashing out not only at school, but at home and just about everywhere else. Amy was only four, but she knew she was hurting others; she only attacked them when there was no one looking. Yes, she had problems, but she *was* acting like a bully and her victim's distress was real enough. In fact, in the first three months of nursery school, Amy had attacked at least five other children verbally and physically.

The mother of the bullied child also recognised that her child had problems. Tim was having difficulty outside the nursery school as well. His mother said that she took him to the Toy Library, where he was pushed over. 'I hadn't even taken off his coat, but it's always like this. Other kids pick on him the whole time. Taking his toys, pulling his hair. Even when I'm there, I can't protect him every second.' Tim is only three and yet he is already a victim of bullying.

Tim was not, however, Amy's only victim. Other children with no apparent problems were singled out by Amy. She just needed someone to pick on because she could not cope.

A father rang our helpline to say that his five-year-old daughter, Julie, had been threatened on the playground by a boy wielding a knife! When he complained that the child with the knife had been readmitted to the school after a brief suspension, he was told that the boy 'had family problems'. The boy was also five years old. Of course this was quite serious and some might not have considered it to be bullying, but classify it as assault. However, it turned out he had been bullying children since the age of three.

The mother of a four-year-old boy was in tears after her son came home covered with mud and sporting a black eye. He had been set upon by a group of five-year-olds and told that he better not tell or they would beat him up again the next day. Fortunately, the nursery school in this case took immediate action and the bullying was nipped in the bud.

If children as young as three or four might become victims and bullies, what can parents do? Is it best to make a big fuss or to leave the children to sort it out? More and more parents are refusing to turn a blind eye to their children's suffering. And, thankfully, more teachers of young children feel strongly that bullying should be taken seriously and stopped from the earliest age.

BULLYING ON THE INCREASE?

If young children are being bullied, is this a new trend or has it always been this bad? The headteacher of a combined nursery and infant school said that the behaviour of children in her schools had definitely changed over the past fifteen years. 'Children are more likely now to lash out at each other and to act out violence on the playground than they were in the past. I see very little ones pretending to be characters from television shows, karate kicking and head butting, instead of playing co-operative games. We make it a point to teach the children to play together – things like skipping ropes, ball games, hopscotch and the like. But I am alarmed that some children deliberately bully others and cannot seem to understand the concept of kindness. If we don't stop them bullying now I think we are laying the foundations for short-term misery now and long-term misery in the future, as well as later adult aggression. After all, versions of the playground heavies and their victims are re-enacted in sitting-rooms and boardrooms daily.'

It makes common sense that tackling bullying issues with young children should eliminate a lot of problems for them as they grow up – both for victims and for bullies.

YOUNG BULLIES

Probably all young children bully once in a while – brothers and sisters, if no one else. I remember saying to my eldest son, then aged six, bullying my youngest, aged three, that no one ever bullied him and that he wasn't going to bully his brother. His response was that his brother 'got away with murder' and he was just trying to set him straight. Nice try, but I wasn't buying it.

Often young children are so intent on getting what they want that they just bowl over anyone in their way. Lisa, aged four, was so excited at her birthday party that she knocked over several children, while racing around opening up presents. She also tried to grab a pass-the-parcel gift won by another child. She wasn't malicious, just a bit over-wrought and perhaps somewhat greedy – a common problem at that age. I wouldn't call Lisa a bully – yet. However, if she isn't taught how to share then we might be looking at a serious problem later on.

Sometimes a young child may go along with the crowd and say or do hurtful things without realising what they are doing or the consequences of their actions. So don't despair if your child appears to be a bully – it may not be as bad as it seems. By quickly stopping the behaviour and explaining why, you will be doing your child a big favour.

While all children need to learn to get along with others, concern about young bullies should be focused more on the child who deliberately sets out to cause distress to another child or who is a danger to other young children, as the child who brought the knife to school mentioned above. Parents should be worried about bullying tendencies if their young children are:

- unable to show any positive feelings towards other children
- unwilling to admit they did anything wrong
- prone to violent tempers
- exhibiting uncontrolled outbursts of bad behaviour
- hurting animals
- feeling already that they are failures at school
- blaming others for their behaviour. (e.g. 'It's his fault I hit him – I didn't like the way he looked at me.')

These are the children who seem to have problems and may share the characteristics outlined in the chapter on bullies in this book.

YOUNG VICTIMS

The under-fives who become victims of bullying are described by their parents as 'sweet' children. These parents have brought up their children to be kind to others and to expect the same in return. When another child is deliberately cruel either by verbally or physically attacking them, they are at a loss. Why would anyone do this to them? That doesn't mean that parents should teach their children to be horrible, but children do need to be warned that not everyone is nice. Perhaps the best way to do this is to tell children that most people in the world like children and most children are kind to others. Some children may be unhappy because they aren't treated well and these children may be cruel to other children because of their misery. Explain to children that if someone bullies them, they've done nothing to deserve it and they should tell you immediately if it happens. Emphasise that it is not their fault if someone bullies them.

From a bully's perspective, a kind child who doesn't make a fuss is an ideal target. The chances are the victim won't fight back and probably won't tell. In a nursery or play group which doesn't tolerate bullying, these children have no problems and that is how it should be. Unfortunately the world is not a perfect place and sometimes the bully gets away with harassing others because the adults are not clued in.

For those children who seem to get bullied no matter where they are – children like Tim – there are different problems. See chapter 2 for ideas about helping these 'perpetual' victims.

PRACTICAL SUGGESTIONS

Bullying is most successful when children don't tell because the bully can carry on as he or she likes. Children need to learn to tell if they are being bullied. To help children both at home and at school, parents can

- stop saying to children that it is wrong to tell tales. Explain that they should always tell if someone is hurting them either verbally or physically.

- make sure that the school their children attend is a 'telling' school. Ask the nursery nurses and teachers to make it clear that bullying is unacceptable. Children have an obligation to *tell* if they are bullied or see bullying take place.

- ensure that the adults do something when they are told. Children must be able to rely on a sympathetic and helpful response if they do tell. In this way they learn that speaking out will make things better; keeping quiet will make things worse.

- offer to monitor the trouble spots at school, like the playground. This may be particularly welcome if lack of staff is a problem.

- use stories, activities, art, etc. to reinforce the anti-bullying messages (see boxes below for ideas).

- arrange for the teachers to put up a photograph of each

child and write something good about the child under the photo. Try just a few words like: A Good Friend or Helps Others or Kind Person or Good to Pets. Change the words once a week and ask the children to help think of good things about each other.

- suggest that children be given stickers or rewards of some sort for 'being nice' to each other. (Sometimes it is difficult to 'catch' a problem child being nice, but it is worth the effort to reinforce good behaviour.) Children will compete to be good if they get recognition. Make sure that every child gets recognised.

- give your own child stickers or rewards for good behaviour.

- organise a 'Kindness Week' and have the children draw posters. Give prizes for the best posters and ribbons or certificates for children being kind to others. Involve as many other parents as possible.

HELPING YOUNG BULLIES

It is possible to help young bullies by recognising that they may be acting that way because they are:

- jealous of another child.
- seeking attention – negative attention is better than none. They may have learned that if they do something bad, they will have everyone's complete attention. Perhaps the rest of the time they are ignored.

- feeling unloved.
- constantly criticised.
- never praised for good behaviour.
- inconsistently disciplined so one day they get away with doing something and the next day they are in trouble for doing the same thing. They cannot figure out how they should act.
- watching too many violent programmes and are acting out what they see.
- expected to be more mature than they are.
- themselves the victims of bullying by family members or other children.
- feeling left out by or different to other children.
- suffering from an undiagnosed medical or learning problem.

In these cases, treating the underlying cause may stop the bullying. For example, a child doing badly who is encouraged to work hard and excel at something – drawing, gymnastics, plasticine modelling, skipping rope, putting together puzzles, racing – may in the process gain enough approval to stop bullying. The younger the child the better chance we have of changing their behaviour. Reforming older chronic bullies is not easy.

If your child is a bully see chapter 3. A brief summary is that you try to:

- remain calm.

- find out the facts.

- talk to the child to find out if she or he is upset or has been bullied and is lashing out as a reaction.

- find out if the child realises that she or he is bullying and hurting someone else – sometimes young children don't know how their actions affect others.

- talk with the parents of the victim, if possible, to set things right and to avoid the bullying carrying on.

- set up a behaviour chart using stars or stickers – give a reward for every five or ten stars but make sure that the time between the good behaviour and the reward is not too great, especially for very young children. For example, some children may need help every hour to behave while others can go for a whole day. The front of the refrigerator is a good place to hang the chart. (Why doesn't someone invent a fridge magnet that actually works?)

- work with the teacher to figure out the best way to help your child.

- talk to the child and explain that, whatever problems there may be, bullying is not the way to solve them.

- control your child's television and video viewing.

- read stories with morals about bullying and talk about them.

- work out a 'behaviour plan' and reward good behaviour.

- arrange a daily or weekly report from the school to home and vice versa.

- ensure that your child apologises and makes amends for the harm caused.

- seek medical, counselling or professional help if your child does not respond after a reasonable time. There may be problems which need to be sorted out before the bullying can be stopped.

Above all, give your child lots of praise and love and *do not label* the child with the name 'bully'. They might be a bully, but we don't want them to start thinking of themselves as bullies or it could become a self-fulfilling prophecy. There is nothing the matter, in my opinion, with saying to young children that you don't like what they did or with labelling the behaviour as bad. I would follow that with telling the child that I know he or she is a good person and will stop the bad behaviour. That's the self-fulfilling prophecy we want.

HELPING YOUNG VICTIMS

Young victims of bullying need help to prevent them from becoming chronic victims in later life. It is sometimes easier to work with them at this age because they are more susceptible to your suggestions than they might be when they are older.

It may be that you have to work around bullies by teaching your child how to cope with threats or how to avoid attracting them in the first place. Also, as I have mentioned in previous chapters, some children seem more prone to bullying than others. This may result from factors beyond their control: the colour of their skin, for example, or some striking physical feature – being above or below average height – that sets them apart from the others. Or it may be that if they are repeatedly bullied, children start acting like victims. If your child is acting like a victim, see chapter 2 for more in-depth ideas, but try helping them to:

- walk tall and straight, in a confident way, rather than hunched over, looking scared and uncertain.

- practise looking in the mirror and saying 'No' or 'Leave me alone' in a clear voice, looking into their own eyes as they say it. A firm rebuff will often deter a bully who is looking for signs of weakness.

- roleplay – something that has been used with great success with young children both in schools and at home. Act out the threatening situation and practise responding calmly but firmly. This type of imaginative play can also help defuse some of the anger that builds up inside children who are persistently bullied.

- ignore the bullying, pretend not to be upset – turn and walk quickly away and tell a grown-up.

- use jokes. It is more difficult to bully a child who refuses to take the bullying seriously. This is especially useful with verbal bullying.

- stay with groups of children, if possible.

- respond to taunts saying the same thing over and over. This is called the broken record approach. For example, a taunt such as 'You've got glasses', tell the child to respond with 'Thank you' and just keep saying it over and over – 'Thank you, thank you.' It is a silly response and it becomes boring for the bully after a while.

In order for children to feel confident using some of these ideas, practise with them and see if they can come up with other ideas. Obviously the ability of the child to try these things depends upon the age and maturity of the child. Adult supervision and intervention with young children is vital.

You can also try to give children confidence by:

- setting up situations where your child will succeed.

- giving them time with you on their own where they have your undivided attention.

- telling the child that you love him or her (bullying makes children feel unlovable).

- doing some special and fun thing together.

- helping them to stop any bad habits which might be contributing to their being bullied.

- encouraging your child to talk and to work out any bad feelings and anger by pounding pegs into one of those little toy workshop benches, drawing pictures, playing with sand, water or plasticine. It is good to bring out their stress instead of letting it wear them down.

As was previously mentioned about bullies, do not label your child as a 'victim'. I use the terms bullies and victims throughout this book because we, as adults, understand the connotations, but with children it is harmful to make them think at this early age that they are 'victims' or 'bullies'. Better to talk about behaviour and how to change it.

If children continue to be bullied or to feel badly about themselves, it may be that counselling would help. Like the chronic bullies, the chronic victims, and sometimes their families, may need some professional guidance to prevent a child from becoming a life-long victim.

THE YOUNGER THE BETTER

One thing is certain, the younger the child, the better chance we have to sort out both the bullies and the victims. There is no need for children to grow up feeling they deserve to be bullied or that bullying others is a good way to behave.

ACTIVITIES FOR YOUNG CHILDREN

Rip-Rip

Give your child a large cut-out figure of a 'child', on A-3 paper (or a smaller one if you can't manage the larger paper).

Explain that the 'child' is a whole, happy person who is going to school one morning feeling good. But during the day other children make comments or do things which make the child feel bad. Ask your child to make a little rip in their cut-out figure every time they think the figure is hurt by something in the story you are going to read out.

This is a very effective way to teach young children empathy.

RIP-RIP STORY

I can't wait to get to school. I know it's going to be fun. Oh, look, here come some other kids.

'Hello, my name is Jane. What's yours?'

What are they saying to me? They said I was ugly and they wouldn't speak to me. **(Rip-Rip)**

Here come some other children. Maybe they'll be friendlier. What are they doing? Oh, they're looking away and pretending not to hear the mean children calling me names. I wish they would do something. I feel so lonely. **(Rip-Rip)**

I guess I'll just play by myself today.

On the playground some of the children wait until no one is looking and then they trip me over. One of them says not to tell or I'll be in trouble. I don't tell. **(Rip-Rip)**

Bullying the Babies

No one will sit with me at lunch. The mean children have told them not to talk to me or eat with me. **(Rip-Rip)**

When my mummy comes to collect me, she asks me if school was fun today. What should I tell her?

You can make up your own story or add or subtract from this one. The children's figures will be in shreds by now. Discuss with them how it feels to be picked on like this and how they could have helped the cut-out child. If teachers use this exercise with the children, they can make a list of the children's suggestions and post it up in the class. This is a good way to remind children how comments and actions can affect people. Children can then be encouraged to make kind comments to each other.

That's my potato!

This works best with two or three children or a small group.

Give each child a potato and ask them to look at it carefully to see things like green marks, spots, its shape, 'eyes', etc. Try to ensure that the potatoes are not completely uniform! They should give their potato a name and make up a story about it:

* What does it do for fun?
* What kinds of food does it like and dislike?
* How old is it?
* Does it have beautiful brothers and sisters? and so on

Ask the children to tell their Potato Story to each other or to you, if you have enough time and not too many children. Then put all the potatoes in a bag, jumble them and put them on a table for the children to come and find their potato. (If the children are likely to disagree, you will have to put a dot or some mark to avoid arguments.)

Explain that it is the small differences that make people individual but they are still all people, just as the potatoes may each be different but they are all still potatoes. Once you take the time to look at someone and really get to know them, you can see that person is not the same as everyone else and that differences are no reason to bully anyone. After all, just because their potato may have three 'eyes' and someone else's potato may have six 'eyes', does that mean that their potato should be singled out for bad treatment?

You may find that your children will not now let you cook their potato! One of my children protected his potato until the darn thing rotted. One way forward is to wait for the 'eyes' to grow and plant it either in the garden or in a pot on the window ledge. Some parents use the potatoes to make those lovely old-fashioned potato prints we made as children. Cut the potato into a shape, dip it in food colouring and print on an old tea towel or piece of paper. Good luck with persuading your children to cut the potato of which they've grown so fond . . .

Drawings

Ask the children to draw a picture of a home, play group or playground where everyone is happy and no one is being bullied. Then ask for a picture in which children are being bullied. Use the pictures to have a discussion about bullying. Display the happy picture on the fridge.

POINTS TO REMEMBER

Very young children can be victims of bullying, just as they can be bullies.

1. The younger the child, the greater the chance of changing bullying behaviour into good behaviour.

2. The emphasis in nursery schools with children should be on learning how to share and be kind to each other.

3. Be concerned if your child says he or she is no good or says they have no friends, or that no one likes them. Your child may be the victim of bullying.

4. Be concerned if your child is oversensitive and easily upset. He or she may become the target of bullies.

5. Teach your child to see the humour in things and to learn how to tease and be teased. This will help protect him or her from bullying. You can start by explaining that your 'pet name' for him or her is a kind of teasing and that people often tease each

other in a loving and fun way. Teach them not to overreact to kind teasing.

6. Note if your child seems upset just before or after going to nursery school, but not at weekends or during holidays. It may be he or she would rather be at home, but it also may be that they are being bullied at nursery school.

7. If your child is aggressive all the time, then you need to either set firmer limits, examine how your child is being treated in the family, find out if there is a medical problem and/or seek counselling.

8. If your child is a bully only at school, make sure that this is the right school for your child and that the children are being properly cared for. Check into the child–teacher ratio and ensure that there is enough supervision and enough for the children to do. Also check to make sure that your child is not responding to being bullied by lashing out at others.

9. Invite children over, to see how your child reacts with them. If your child is bullying, act out with him or her how to be nice to other children. If your child is being bullied, either cut off the relationship with the bully if there is only one, or note whether your child is the victim of lots of children and may need help to build up self-esteem (see chapter 4) or how to make friends (see chapter 5).

10. Beware the adage that young children don't bully, they just tease each other. Remember that once teasing hurts one child, it is no longer teasing but bullying.

8

BULLYING AND THE FAMILY

When ten-year-old Megan was being bullied at school it affected her entire family. Instead of withdrawing to herself as many children who are bullied do, Megan started bullying her younger brothers and sister. Megan's mother told me that Megan would come home from school in an 'evil mood and make life hell for everyone'.

Overnight she turned from being the laughing, charming child who was a pleasure to be around into a snarling, snapping creature. She slammed doors, picked on the little ones, burst into tears for no reason and was generally a terror. I couldn't believe it. The problem was made worse by the fact that my husband and I started fighting about everything. We disagreed about how to discipline her, what we should do about the bullying and how we should handle our other children.

My husband thought that Megan was being a sissy and that she should just stand up to the bullies and tell them to get lost (or words to that effect!). I felt that the school should deal with it as Megan was the victim of a gang of kids who were out of control. We could not even bring up the subject of bullying without arguing. This went on for several weeks until we were all a mass of nerves and screaming at each other and the children. It all came to a head when Megan ran away from school one day and we couldn't find her for several hours. We were frantic with worry and called the police.

They took it all very seriously and found her sobbing, sitting near the school playground. Thank goodness. When the police brought her home late that evening she and we were red-eyed from crying. Her father and I sat up half the night with her, talking about all the things we should have been talking about all along. We agreed that we would ring the teacher and headteacher in the morning and make an appointment to all go in and figure out a way to end this torment.

My husband saw how distressed Megan was and agreed that it was impossible for her to stand up to these little thugs. We had to convince him that he couldn't go and 'sort them and their parents out' or he might get arrested. He was that angry. I guess the fear of losing Megan finally made us sit up and take notice that we could not let this bullying go on destroying our family.

Megan's parents faced a common problem that is not often talked about – bullying does affect the entire family. This is true whether the bullying is outside the family and/or in it. In Megan's case, the bullying was brought into the family by the victim. She could not cope with what was happening and knew that eventually her parents would figure out a way to help her. She didn't plan to become a bully, but she was so unhappy that she lashed out at the people she loved because she was so miserable.

EVERYONE AFFECTED

Don't think that every bullied child comes home and starts bullying others, as Megan did. Although it does happen frequently, many children who are bullied just withdraw or feel depressed and do not lash out at others. In fact, they often turn on themselves, blaming themselves for being bullied. Regardless of how the victims of bullying react in their own families, the fact is that the bullying of a child does affect everyone in the family.

One mother told me that the entire time her child was at school she found herself watching the clock. 'I would look at the time and think about where he was. If it was lunch time, the minutes would seem like hours because I knew that was a time he was bullied. I would breathe a sigh of relief when lunch was over, but worry again during playtime and when it was time to come home. I just could not relax until he walked in the door. Even then I braced myself before asking him how his day was.'

In some cases, families are unfortunate enough to have a bully in their midst who is not being bullied elsewhere. This child or adult has problems or has been brought up to think that they can behave this way. The parents watch the clock dreading the time when the bullying child will come in to make life difficult for the other children. But what I find especially sad is when the bully is one of the parents and the children are trapped in what I would call an abusive situation.

DEALING WITH THE EFFECTS

Let's start with children like Megan and how to deal with this spin-off of school bullying. If you are having trouble agreeing about what to do:

- remember that many couples have dramatically different ideas about how to raise children and deal with specific issues. One parent may favour a laid-back approach, while the other is setting high standards and being demanding. In Megan's case, one parent thought that children should be tough and deal with problems themselves, the other felt that the adults should step in and solve the problem,

- think about how much it will hurt your child if you cannot figure out a united way to tackle the bullying.

- realise that by agreeing to work together, you will reduce the tension all your children are feeling and most likely stop your child from bullying brothers and sisters (and parents!).

- remember that if you do not act the bullying will never stop and might get worse because your child will have no positive support.

If there is one message I could get to all parents of bullied children, it would be that bullying does affect the whole family and you will have to work to put that right. How?

101 Ways to Deal with Bullying

- Tell your child that you will work to stop the bullying.

- Don't be put off by the school or anyone else labelling you as an 'hysterical' parent because you are standing up for your child. If you don't stand up for her or him, who will? (See chapter 6 Working with the School.)

- Set firm limits. Talk to your child and explain that you know she or he is angry and frustrated and hurt by the bullying, but that you will not allow them to behave badly.

- Keep some flexibility. This may seem at odds with the suggestion directly above. But what I mean here is that your child may be hurting so much that there will be times when you have to cut him or her some slack. This doesn't mean allowing the child to beat up brothers and sisters, but forgive the slammed door or ignore the angry remark when you know your child has reached his or her limits. Kids get frustrated and it has to come out somewhere.

- Explain that you understand that your child may be angry and that you think it is OK to be angry. Then work out some ways your child can express that anger without bullying others in the family:

  * keep a diary and write down all your feelings

  * draw pictures

  * take time to cool down – leave the room if you are starting to take your anger out on others

166

* get a punch bag and hit it

* take up a sport and get lots of exercise

* ring a helpline (see Help Organisations)

* talk to a friend

* write a book about bullying. Make sure the victim is the hero or heroine

* make models out of plasticine and take your anger out on them instead of your family.

● Find things about your child to praise.

● Don't label your child a bully. Say you know that your child is not like this and that he or she is acting badly because you know they are unhappy. It is a relief for children to know that you see through their 'badness' and have faith in them.

● If you find yourself shouting or overreacting, leave the room, count to ten, have a cup of tea or call a friend and talk – anything to get back into control. It is awful enough to endure bullying without having us parents making things worse.

● Try not to feel guilty because you couldn't protect your child from bullying. Heaven knows that it is natural to be upset and feel powerless when trying to cope with a bullying, but the bullying is not your fault, it is the fault of the bully.

- Give your child the same message about guilt – the bullying is not your child's fault.

- If your child wishes, sign him or her up for either self-defence or martial arts classes with the local authority or a private organisation. Be sure that the class is designed to improve self-confidence and not to turn out ruffians. Most reputable teachers of these kinds of courses emphasise the building of self-esteem and the proper use of the martial arts. Many bullied children have benefited from such activities.

- Find other activities your child might want to do like take up a musical instrument or a hobby, or maybe join a youth club or scouting group. These activities may give your child other friends away from the school.

- Sports are important for all children, but especially for kids who don't feel very good about themselves. Succeeding in sport will make them feel more confident. It does not have to be a team sport. I am still amazed at those shools which allow the 'team captain' to choose his or her team, leaving the less-wanted children until last. How utterly insensitive can you get and what a good way to ensure that kids hate team sports! Anyway, your child might like to try running, swimming, cycling, tennis, bowling or other sports. I think this is an excellent way to relieve anxieties and to find new skills. Also it gives the rest of the family a break!

- If you are still at odds with your partner about how to handle the bullying, negotiate and agree that you both want the bullying to stop. Work out a plan even if you take some actions separately.

In Megan's case, her father worked on building up Megan's confidence but did not insist that she fight back. It would have been foolish to insist on this as the bullies would have hurt Megan even more, and in this case nothing would have been accomplished. Megan took up swimming and enrolled in a dance class. Her father took her to the swimming baths and gave her lots of praise for her accomplishments.

Megan's mother, with her husband's backing, talked to the teachers and they agreed to quietly catch the bullies at it so that Megan would not be seen as a grass. The bullies were bullying other children, so Megan was not the sole victim.

Both parents laid down the law with Megan about her behaviour towards her siblings and them. If she was angry, then she could talk to her parents, or write in her diary or listen to music. But she could not hit her siblings or bully them or act like a brat. Megan could not necessarily retreat to her room as she shared it with her sister.

For Megan the bullying problem was eventually solved. Her family are now bracing themselves for the normal teenage years ahead!

WHEN A CHILD IS WITHDRAWN OR DEPRESSED

If your child is being bullied and is reacting by withdrawing and being miserable, this will affect your family as well. You can use many of the suggestions above, but you may also want to try:

- planning successful and enjoyable experiences for your child. I am talking about simple things which make your child feel OK. Take your child to the cinema or to a play. Let him or her choose and ask them to help you find your way there. Go to a restaurant or fast-food chain and ask them to order the food. Basically you are building a little confidence each time they succeed in even something as small as combing their hair in a nice way. The object is to bring a smile to their faces.

- getting them to make decisions. This can be about what they wear, what you have for dinner, what kind of a cake you bake for Gran's birthday, where you place a picture on the wall. It is a sad fact that bullied kids may feel so powerless that even these little decisions are difficult for them.

- giving them ways to deal with put-downs. If another child is picking on one particular thing, think of ways to counteract the problem. It may be that they could make a joke or walk away and pretend not to hear or just look blank.

- asking them to watch how other kids deal with put-downs or insults. It might give them some clues about what to do.

- using the assertiveness notes in chapter 2, How to Help Victims.

- seeking help from a counsellor or the organisations listed in the back of this book. Don't let a child wallow in depression. If you can't pull them out of it, get advice.

None of this means that I think children should put up with put-downs or bullying. But children who are really upset and withdrawn because of bullying need practical ways to help themselves while you are dealing with the problem.

We have to remember children who are also angry. Like Megan they may turn the anger on those people they know will love them no matter what or they may turn the anger inwards. They are also lonely and frightened, and parents may be the only ones who care enough to help, and to absorb some of their pain.

BULLIES IN THE FAMILY

You may be 'blessed' with an extremely active child who reacts to everything in an intense way. He or she may be so keen to get on with what they want to do that they literally knock over the other children in the family so they can charge onwards and upwards. In this case your child may not be so much a bully as a child in need of limits and boundaries. These children need help in controlling their behaviour and rules that are stated, written and enforced. Otherwise they may end up bullying other children and not just their siblings. See chapter 2, How to Help Bullies, and try:

- channelling your child's energy and excitement into activities he or she can do alone, such as swimming, running, painting, building models.

- ensuring that your child develops empathy with other children. Read stories (see Resources), discuss films and videos and news stories as they come up; ask your child how he or she thinks people feel when they are hurt or sad.

- staying as calm as possible when correcting behaviour. Don't shout, humiliate or hit your child. This will only make him or her more hyper and less able to take in what you are saying.

- explaining the limits and consequences during a quiet time. Then, if your child bullies siblings, put the consequences into effect immediately. No arguments, just firm limits.

WRONG CULPRIT

It does happen that parents punish the wrong child for bullying. Children who are bullying are very adept at niggling and when the other child reacts, they can act like innocent little lambs. Take the case of Ben:

James, aged six, and Ben, his nine-year-old brother, were sitting at the kitchen table. James was drawing while Ben was building a fort out of Lego. No one else was in the room. Ben moved over next to James. He ignored Ben and moved over to get away. Ben pushed his fort onto James's work. 'Get off,' said James, annoyed but still doing his drawing. Ben, who wanted attention, picked up a piece of Lego and threw it at James. James shoved him away. Ben threw more pieces and then stuck his finger into James's lip. James grabbed his hand and bit it. Ben screamed. Mum rushed in. Seeing Ben's hand, she yelled at James. She then comforted Ben, saying to James: 'You are a very naughty boy.' Here Ben had been annoying and even bullying, but James has got the blame. James shouldn't have bitten him, but Ben clearly needs to know what's likely to happen if he continues bugging someone. Sometimes the rough justice of children works better than anything we can do. James, being the elder by three years, should not be picking on his younger brother.

This was an unfair situation for the younger boy. The lessons for us as parents is that fighting or bullying in the family is never simple – there are always undercurrents, only some of which we can fathom out.

STRATEGIES

In my experience, parents need strategies for when your nerves are at full stretch and one child is bullying another. You cannot just bow out and let one of your children be bullied by another. I suggest that parents:

1. Be specific

Give very specific instructions like: 'Do not touch his car'; 'Stop that behaviour this instant'; 'Do not hit'; 'Leave the room'. Children do not respond to 'be nice', especially if they are angry.

2. Arrange a place for possessions

Sometimes children take something that belongs to someone else and a 'blood feud' develops which leads to bullying. Find a place for each child's toys and games which is their own. Ideally, give each a lockable box to keep special things in. This makes it clear that some things are their own and helps if you have to sort out a dispute.

3. Give kids ideas

Give children strategies. Ten-year-old Sam went berserk every time his sister said 'Sam is a sissy.' She loved winding him up. Sam's mum helped him work out things to say which made him feel less tense so his sister couldn't 'get to him'. He came up with 'Buzz off, elephant breath.' His mum got him to try: 'I love you, too' and 'Yes . . . all great men are sissies' or 'Twinkle, twinkle, little star . . . what you say is what you are.'

4. Stay out of it, if possible

Keep out of the 'everyday' fights as much as possible. If you only seem to give them attention when they fight, try giving them attention only when they don't fight.

5. Recognise frustration

But you can make it less awful. When one of them says: 'I hate her', say: 'Yes, you hate her right now. You don't have to like everyone all the time.' If you tell them, 'You don't mean that really; you love your sister', you'll just create more anger.

6. Separate them

Prise them apart. When things look nasty try 'time out' in different rooms (if you can separate them); threaten withdrawal of pocket money (for both) unless they cool down.

7. Find out the basic problem

Take them aside individually and find out if there is a basic reason for continual bullying – something that just keeps niggling away at them.

8. Discover if there is a time for bullying

See if there's a time when your child bullies most often: it may be bedtime, bath time, or when visitors come. It may be when you go out or leave for work. It may be when they watch television.

One mother found that her son, aged fourteen, was a real bully over the television. He always demanded the other children watch what he wanted and if they resisted, he either hit them or pushed them out of the room. She talked with the children and laid down rules about when, where and what they were to do about television. The bullying stopped.

9. Avoid labelling

Don't tell your child that he or she is a bully or say it in front of others. It becomes a self-fulfilling prophecy. ('That's what I do best – bully!')

10. Allow anger

Allow children to be angry – safely. I invite them to draw awful pictures of each other – then they know you understand that they are angry and they learn that drawing is a better way to vent anger than hitting.

11. Use humour

I think humour is a great weapon that parents should use as often as possible. A flippant remark can work better than a long analysis: 'Listen here, Bossy Boots, I'm in charge!' The problem is trying to be humorous when you want to kill them!

12. Notice good behaviour

If you can, catch your children when they aren't bullying. Some days it may not seem possible, but there will be times when they are little angels.

13. Undo bad deals

Life is all about giving and getting a good enough deal. Kids learn this from an early age and practise it relentlessly. Needless to say, this can also lead to bullying behaviour on the part of the wiser child.

Harry, six, is hysterical. 'I want it back,' he sobs repeatedly. 'It isn't fair.' Rebecca, his twelve-year-old sister, walks in, steps over his sobbing form, and calmly ignores her brother.

'Give it back,' yells Harry.

'No,' says Rebecca, very coolly and decisively. 'We made a deal.'

'What deal?' asks her father, deeply suspicious.

'He swapped his basketball with me and now he wants it back. I gave him three stickers that glow in the dark. It was a deal and we shook hands on it. Now he wants his ball back and that's not fair.' Rebecca is confident that her case is totally airtight.

'The stickers definitely aren't as good as my ball.' Harry is furious.

'But we shook on it and you can't go back on a deal.'

They look at you expectantly. The ball is worth £15; the stickers 50p. Rebecca knows this. Harry doesn't but he feels wronged. The good child-rearing books say you should talk with the children individually and get all the facts. Then democratically ask them to help you sort it out.

Rebecca's dad hasn't the time or patience to do that. Anyway he knows this is a try-on by Rebecca.

'It's not fair,' he pronounces, 'the deal's off.'

14. Sort out power struggles

Power struggles are the basis of so many bullying problems, for kids and adults. At some stage, we need to teach children to exercise power and fairness at the same time. I feel we need to talk with our children about the subject of power. It's a subject they take very personally. Help your children by:

- asking them to understand that everyone has power – even a little baby (if only to burst your eardrums). We have power over children; an employer has power over you; and children have power over brothers/sisters, other children, pets.

- playing 'what if' games relating to power:

  o What would you do if you knew someone in the playground was picking on a much younger child?

  o What would you do if I made a deal with you that wasn't fair?

  o What would you do if someone swapped £100 for a toy of yours and then wanted it back? Would it matter how much the toy was worth? It could be worth (a) £4 (b) £100 (c) £200.

  o What would you do if you made a deal with your best friend and he/she changed his/her mind? Would it make a difference how long it took before she changed her mind (a) two minutes after the deal? (b) ten minutes after the deal? (c) a week later?

Out of this, agree ground rules for 'deals' which include a cooling-off time, during which either party can back out.

What we want children to learn is that there is a way to use power so that people are not taken advantage of. Misusing power causes unhappiness.

15. Apologise, make amends

Children need to learn that it is not OK to bully someone and then just pretend nothing happened. Ben needed to apologise to James for interfering with his drawing. If he had ruined it then Ben should have made amends in the best way he could – maybe by getting James a fresh piece of paper or doing some of James's chores. There is no need to humiliate a child, but a simple 'I'm sorry' makes the victim feel better and the bully think about what he or she has done. Taking responsibility and feeling ashamed of bad behaviour helps a child to learn from his or her mistakes and is a giant step towards stopping bullying.

16. Some other ideas

If the bullying continues, try:

- confiscating whatever it is that they are fighting over. If it is a television programme, turn off the television.

- physically restrain them, if necessary, but don't hit them. Hitting only proves to them that it is valid to use force to end arguments.

- putting the bully into a room by him or herself to cool off and making yourself a cup of tea and thinking pleasant thoughts such as where you are going to go on your summer holidays ALONE.

- finding out both sides of the story and making a judgement and telling them that it is finished and over. No more discussion.

- at a quiet time, involving your child or children in finding a long-term solution to ongoing fights. For example, if the bullying is always about who got the bigger share, do what my aunt who had six children always did: make the children themselves divide the portions. Whoever divides gets last pick. Take turns dividing and picking. I watched my cousins take incredible care to fill the glasses exactly or cut the cake with medical precision. My sister and I were made to do the same – it kept us interested and quiet while we measured to the very last drop.

- taking away a privilege if there are consequences needed. Agree which privileges might have to go if the child continues to bully. He or she might decide it isn't worth it!

- teaching children that they can use words to sort out disagreements, instead of bullying to get their own way. They may actually need examples from you and practise. Starting sentences with 'I don't agree with you' is better than 'You're dumb' or worse. If you find your children are repeating your words when you fight with your spouse or partner, you might have to tone down or change your own way of arguing and that's not easy! If possible, take them along to listen to a debate so they can see how issues can be talked about and argued out without fisticuffs or other bullying behaviour.

PARENTS AS BULLIES

It is so difficult to help a child when one parent is a bully and the other parent will not step in to help the child. If your child is being bullied by a parent, please stand up for your child or you will find that your child not only feels abused by the bullying parent, but abandoned by the parent who will not help. Try to get the bully to:

- listen to how he or she talks to the child – do they shout, bark orders, threaten or humiliate your child? If so, this should be pointed out to the bully. Tape record it if he or she doesn't believe you and then play it back when the child is not around. Sometimes just hearing how awful it sounds brings a person to his or her senses.

- look at his or her behaviour – do they arbitrarily change the rules so your child never knows what will happen next? If so, I think this is a power issue with the bully. Only the bully knows the rules and that keeps the child guessing and worried. Children need to know what the rules are and what will happen if the rules are broken. Of course the rules need to be reasonable, as well. A rule that a fifteen-year-old can never go out with friends is not only unreasonable, it is cruel.

- examine if there is a way for your child to air grievances with him or her. Children need to be able to say to their parents that they think something is unjust or that they are not being treated fairly. If your child has no way to do this, then the grievances will fester and result in problems for the child and the whole family.

- take responsibility for changing his or her behaviour. This may mean taking a parenting course or contacting one of the parenting organisations listed at the end of this book (see Resources). It may mean reading about ways to communicate with children (and, I suspect, other people). It may mean family and individual counselling.

If the bullying parent is not willing to consider how he or she is harming your child, you may need to make a choice between that person and the welfare of your child. For a child to live with a powerful, bullying adult who undermines the child's self-worth and confidence is emotional abuse. For a child to be subjected to this kind of abuse over the years while growing up is, in my opinion, unforgivable.

POINTS TO REMEMBER

If I had to choose ten suggestions for dealing with family bullying, they would be:

1. set limits and consequences for children. If they bully or behave badly, they suffer the consequences.

2. but also praise children when they're being good. This is hard to remember to do, but it works wonders.

3. remember that everyone in the family is affected if a child is being bullied and that the family may need time to heal even after the bullying stops. Try to plan fun things to do together and ways to relax. Don't always focus on the bullying.

4. make everyone laugh by doing something completely absurd. It is so embarrassing to have your parents do something like cluck around the kitchen imitating a chicken that the children may well forget about the pain for a while.

5. teach all children to be effective with words instead of fists or put-downs. Give them specific, clever things they can say when a sibling (or another child) bullies or taunts them. For example, if Gary can always get a rise from Celia by calling her 'stupid', Celia could be taught to say 'thank

you' and walk away. Of course, Gary needs to be told off, as well!

6. help children to get their anger out. It's all right to be angry with someone if there is cause. It's how you deal with that anger that gets you into difficulty. Teach children to state why they are angry and what they want to happen. Then give them strategies for coping with anger so it doesn't eat them up inside or spill out into bickering or bullying. Writing letters, drawing angry pictures about the other person, thumping away on the piano, or pounding nails into a board might help.

7. try to let the children sort it out, if possible. But intervene if one child is really getting the short end of the stick. After all, that's why kids have parents.

8. find ways to help the bullied child – this will help the family. Channel anger and energies into sports, music, drama, art, hobbies, clubs or anything that will give your child a better feeling about him or herself and give the family a break, as well.

9. take time out for yourself (see chapter 9, Taking Care of Yourself). If you are stressed, all the children will suffer including the child who is being bullied.

10. find a quiet time to involve the family in finding solutions to the problem. Explain what is happening and ask for their understanding and co-operation.

You may need to say that 'Will is being bullied at school and that is why he and we are so upset and unhappy.' Then go from there. Be sure to include Will in the decision to have a family consultation. You may find that things improve dramatically at home because everyone is trying harder to pitch in and make life easier.

9

TAKING CARE OF YOURSELF

Gayle was a thirty-four-year-old mother of three children. Her ex-husband, Alan, had left her for another woman. He took no interest in their children, nor did he help when Gayle rang to say that their youngest son, Paul, aged ten, was being bullied at school. Alan's response was, 'You're obviously bringing the lad up to be a wimp. Get him some boxing lessons.' Alan then hung up.

Gayle worked full-time, kept the home running smoothly, took the children to their various clubs and lessons, helped them with their homework and fell into bed exhausted every night. She was a basket case by the time she came to see me. The poor woman could not summon up the energy to help her bullied child. It was just one bridge too far and she couldn't cross it. She was desperate to help Paul, but we had to help her find a few ways to unwind and give herself a mental break before she could tackle Paul's problem.

To add to all the things Gayle was coping with, the staff at the school decided that the real problem was that Gayle, being a divorced working mother, was not spending enough time with her children, hence Paul was being bullied! They also told her that she was a 'hysterical parent' because she demanded that the school do something to stop the bullying. Her reasoning was that Paul had not been bullied before and that he wasn't being bullied at home so the problem was a school-based one. She was right.

As another parent, Jay, in a similar situation said, 'Darn right — I *am* a hysterical parent. No one seems to care about what is happening, so I have no choice. Who else is going to feel this strongly and be trying to protect my child if not me. I don't care what you call me, but I will fight for my child!' To further complicate Jay's case, he himself was bullied as a child and the bullying of his daughter brought back lots of angry memories. In fact, a survey by the National Confederation of Parent Teacher Associations found that parents who were bullied at school were more than twice as likely to have children who have been subjected to bullying.[1]

Unfortunately, the cases of Gayle and Jay are not unusual. Many parents of bullied children find themselves unable to cope because of the stress, regardless of whether they are single, living with someone or married. In Gayle's case, the stress was exacerbated by all the other things she had to deal with in her life. In Jay's case, the added guilt he felt because he had not been able to protect his child from the suffering he endured made it more difficult to cope. But even if there are two parents and neither has been bullied, the disagreements about how things should be handled often lead to unholy rows which make the situation worse for everyone including the child. Father may want the child to fight back or stand up to the bully, mother may expect the school to sort it out. Whatever you do, avoid getting all the other relatives involved.

There is no doubt that sooner or later all parents go through times of anxiety and stress. That comes with the territory. I confess that there have been times when I have just wanted to forget the whole parenthood business and find a quiet corner to curl up in with a good book, even though my children have not had to deal with horrible bullying. Basically it is a fairly normal reaction to want to go back to times when you only had to worry about yourself. But combine that with all the strains that Gayle or Jay were experiencing, add a bullied child to the mix and you have a parent near to breaking.

It is vital that parents of children who are being bullied or who are bullying others find a way to cope so that they can help their children. What I am about to suggest is in no way frivolous. When Gayle came to see me, we worked out some of the ways she could find a little time for herself so she could recharge her depleted batteries.

Of course Gayle or Jay could not do all these things. No one can. But you can choose to try some of the things if you are at your wits' end. Many of these ideas come from a book I wrote for parents, called *501 Ways to Being a Good Parent*, so you can see that all parents need to relax even if their children are not being bullied.

1. Escape to the park

Take thirty minutes, go to the park, sit on a bench and watch the people go by. Better yet, lie on the grass and watch the clouds.

2. Take a class

Sign up for a class with your local authority. Learn a new language, how to sing, play an instrument, sew, cook, type, become computer literate – you name it, they've got it and it is cheap or even free. Perhaps it will seem an extra burden

because you have to find the time, but if you don't give yourself some time, you may crack.

3. Visualisation

If you can't get out of the house at all, try visualisation. A psychotherapist friend of mine, Dr Brian Roet, uses this technique which can relax you in minutes. When I asked him to try it out on me, I was surprised and delighted with the results:

o Close your eyes and think where in your body you might feel happy. Let's say you choose your chest.

o Visualise going inside your chest and seeing the happy feeling. Think in colour and see what colour the feeling is. Let's say you choose yellow and red as the colours.

o Visualise what the feeling looks like. Is it crystals, softly lapping water, clouds, snow, raindrops, etc.? Let's say you decide that your happy feeling is crystals and they are yellow and red. Look at those sparkling crystals and try to visualise them even brighter yellow and red – so that they shine and glimmer.

o So you now have a happy feeling associated with colours and crystals. When you are feeling stressed, close your eyes and think of those crystals and relax.

This may sound a bit hocus-pocus, but it only takes a few minutes and it works wonders. It is also something you can help your children to do when they are feeling anxious about

191

being bullied or some other problem. A friend of mine said her child had a teacher who really did not like him. The teacher didn't appreciate his sense of humour or his personality. In fact, they were like chalk and cheese. Her son calmed himself before this class by visualising coloured crystals. I think he may have visualised the teacher with coloured crystals on her head, but he never admitted to that. Anyway, when things get on top of you, try it. I think you'll like it.

4. Start or join a parents' group

It is no accident that groups of parents end up being friends because their children know each other or because their children have all had problems of the same kind. It is a major way of staying sane to realise that you are not alone as the parents of children who are being bullied. There really is comfort in exchanging experiences and ideas.

Ring the helplines listed in the back of this book and ask if they know of any other parents in your area who might like to talk or meet. Some areas already have a group going. Other areas are waiting for the right person to come along to start one.

5. Treat yourself

Go out for scones and tea, or lunch. Take a friend and discuss anything except children. Try hard to keep the conversation away from problems. You need a rest from them once in a while, at least.

6. Go to the cinema

Most cinemas have cheap tickets before 3.00 p.m. and some have certain days when films cost next to nothing. Find out and, if you're a parent who is at home, take yourself to the cinema in the middle of the day. If you work outside the home, prevail upon a friend to look after the kids and go on a Saturday afternoon.

7. Take a peaceful walk

Go for a walk, pack a picnic and find a nice place to have a peaceful lunch.

8. Enjoy a luxurious bath

Pour a bubble bath, close the door and announce to everyone that you are not to be disturbed for half an hour. Try it by candlelight with a glass of wine, it's heaven! You cannot deny yourself this – everyone has to keep clean. Just indulge yourself a bit and take time.

9. Do something different

Go swimming, have a sauna, sit in a Jacuzzi, go ice-skating or roller-skating. It is a good way to clear your head and you may find you can deal much better with your child's problems.

10. Garden for fun

If you are lucky enough to have a garden or a balcony or even a window box, dig around and plant something. But only do this if it is fun and not because the garden needs doing. Then it's a chore instead of an escape.

11. Relieve that tension

Really treat yourself – have a massage or a facial. This could count as one of the greatest pleasures of all as all the stress is soothed out by an expert.

12. Go on a journey

Pick a village that is accessible by train, buy a day return ticket and go wandering around exploring the shops, museums and ancient buildings. Treat yourself to lunch, as well.

13. Read

Curl up with a good book, ignore all the work waiting to be done and immerse yourself.

14. Write

Put aside an hour a day and begin that book you've always known you have inside you. If you wrote one page each day, by the end of the year you would have 365 pages.

15. Draw

Get a sketch book and start drawing or painting. Even if you think you have 'no talent' it focuses your mind on other things besides the fun and games of parenthood.

16. Be creative

Try pottery. I tried this once and ended up with a blob of useless clay and dirty fingernails. However, for those with patience and talent, it is very satisfying to make something and a great escape.

17. Sleep

Not very exciting, I know, but if you feel stressed and exhausted, then sleep when your kids sleep, if they are young. If not, take a nap when they are at school. You will be a better parent if you aren't in a zombie-like state. The best advice about this was from Stephanie, a mother of four, who said, 'Take a hot bubble bath, get your favourite book and teddy bear and go to bed. Read until your eyes can't stay open, cuddle the teddy bear and sleep for two hours.' Sounds wonderful, doesn't it?

18. Axe the guilt

I realise that there is a well of guilt when you think about enjoying yourself while your child is suffering. Think of it this way – if you don't give yourself some time, you may fall apart when your child needs you most. I consider this kind of self-care to be in the best interests of your child. If it helps, use visualisation to swallow up any guilt you are feeling.

19. Take your child or children and go

No, I don't mean to vanish for ever. But a weekend away with friends or relatives or in a tent in a campsite may give everyone a much-needed break and help you to bond as a family to give you strength to beat the bullying.

20. Get help

If all else fails and you cannot find a way to cope or relax, do get help. Ring the KIDSCAPE helpline or talk to a friend. Seek professional help for yourself or your family. Whatever you do, don't just sit back and let the bullying reduce you to a dishrag and destroy your family. You don't deserve this!

From talking with thousands of parents who have had to deal with their children being bullied or being bullies, I know that it is one of the most stressful problems because it never seems to be straightforward. You often seem to take one step forward while taking two steps backwards.

Of course you will spend 99.9% of your time trying to ensure that the bullying goes away and your child feels safe and confident. Just don't forget yourself on the way.

POINTS TO REMEMBER

1. A relaxed parent is better able to cope with a bullied or bullying child.

2. Parents deserve time for themselves.

3. Find out about opportunities in your area that you could take advantage of and might enjoy.

4. Talk to your child's other parent and try to work out a common plan to help your child. Dissension helps no one.

5. Don't let anyone label you as a hysterical parent or make you feel guilty for helping your child.

6. If you were bullied at school, try to divorce your feelings about what happened to you from what is happening to your child.

7. If you spend time taking care of yourself, it will make it much easier to help your child deal with the bullying.

8. You may have to help yourself and your other children if one child in your family is being bullied. Bullying affects the entire family. You may bear the brunt of the entire family's misery, as the bullied child lashes out at brothers and sisters and parents because of the pain he or she is experiencing. That extra few minutes you take

for yourself may make the difference between you being able to cope with the bullying 'fall-out'.

9. Nearly 60% of the parents surveyed by the National Confederation of Parent Teacher Associations had children who had been bullied.[2] If your child is being bullied, sadly, you are not alone. Try to join with other parents for help and support when approaching the school or trying to reduce your own stress.

10. If you find that you cannot cope or use any of the suggestions for relaxing, get help. Don't just let the bullying ruin you and your family.

1 Edwards, Lynne 'Echoes of Bullying' commissioned by the National Confederation of Parent Teacher Associations, 1996.
2 ibid.

10

LEGAL RIGHTS AND RESPONSIBILITIES

Twelve-year-old Eric was walking home from his after-school soccer club when he was approached by three boys from another school. They punched and kicked him, then ran off leaving him bleeding on the ground. Eric needed three stitches over his eye. He was bruised and sore for a week.

Fourteen-year-old Astrid was followed off the school bus by four older girls. They taunted her, wrenched her arm behind her back and pushed her down on the ground. They left, taking her school bag with them. Astrid was off school for several days with her injuries.

Eleven-year-old Max was confronted by another boy, Peter, at the end of a play practice in the school theatre. Peter was jealous of Max, and thought Max was conceited and stuck up because of his leading role in the school play. After a few harsh words, Peter thumped Max so hard that Max fell off the stage and broke his arm.

Fifteen-year-old Anthony was a popular boy with lots of friends. The school bullies had tried to make his life miserable, but Anthony just laughed and walked away. The bullies taunted him because his father was the local minister. His father rang KIDSCAPE to say that Anthony had been tripped in the school lunch room by the bullies and had broken his nose. The school refused to call the police and said the minister should 'forgive the bullies because they were troubled youths'.

Bullying is not a criminal offence. But, as the Children's Legal Centre says in their excellent leaflet 'Bullying: A Guide to the Law' (see Help Organisations), 'some forms of bullying may amount to criminal behaviour. When a child has been assaulted either physically or sexually, the bullies may have committed the criminal offence of common assault or indecent assault.'

In all of the cases mentioned above, the bullies were over the age of ten, which is the age of criminal responsibility. KIDSCAPE recommends that the police be called in cases where a child has sustained injuries. If the bullies are allowed to get away with this kind of assault when they are young, then the chances are they will go on to commit even worse crimes when they are older.

In all of these cases the law has been broken. Depending upon the extent of their injuries, Eric, Astrid, Max and Anthony had offences committed against them which could be prosecuted under Criminal Law.

Actual Bodily Harm (ABH) encompasses the victims being bruised, cut or bleeding.

Grievous Bodily Harm (GBH) encompasses broken bones, severe bruising or hospital treatment.

The police cannot make a charge without some sort of evidence that an assault has taken place and that the culprit is responsible for the assault.

If your child is assaulted in this way:

1. take your child to a doctor or the hospital

2. ensure that there is a record kept of medical evidence of the assault

3. contact the police

4. ask your child to write down everything he or she can remember about the bullying incidents leading up to the assault. This should be done immediately after the assault, if possible.

We have found that schools which were reluctant to take action in cases such as Max and Anthony do become more co-operative when the parents bring in the police. In my opinion there should be no hesitation on the part of the school to bring in the police when a child is deliberately injured to the extent that it is ABH or GBH under Criminal Law.

Children and young people can also be victims of assault:

Brian, aged thirteen, was persistently harassed and tormented by a group of girls and boys his own age. They called him names, wrote rude things about him on the chalkboard, threatened him with beatings if he dared to come to school, and sent him letters telling him that he would be killed.

Christine, aged twelve, was constantly bullied by a gang of fifteen-year-olds. They vandalised her bicycle, told her that they would stab her if she showed her face in the lunch room and sent her nasty notes saying she was ugly and fat and suggested that she kill herself to 'save the world from her hideous body'. On the playground the gang made gestures of cutting their throats every time they could get away with it. Christine had a breakdown and refused to go to school.

A person does not have to suffer physical injuries to be assaulted. **Assault** is defined as:

1. the intentional application of force to the person of another without his consent, or the *threat* of such force by act or gesture.

2. any act which constitutes any *attempt, offer* or *threat* to use violence or any unlawful force to the person of another.

WHAT ABOUT THE CULPRITS?

The law states that children over the age of ten can be found guilty of a criminal offence:

1. Under-Tens

   Children under the age of ten are immune from prosecution. They are not old enough to be held criminally responsible for their actions. However, the police can make out a charge sheet, which may deter the child in the future. In extreme cases, the child can be taken into local authority care.

2. Ten to Fourteen

   Children in this age range can be deemed to be legally responsible for their actions, but it must be established that they knew they were doing something wrong. These children will be tried in juvenile court, not in a criminal court.

3. Fourteen to Under Seventeen

   Young people in this age range will be held accountable for their actions. The defence that they did not know they were doing something wrong no longer holds. They are tried in juvenile court and can be sentenced to young offenders institutions if found guilty of a serious offence.

SCHOOLS' RESPONSIBILITIES

Schools are not required by law to have a written disciplinary policy about bullying. However, the Education Act 1996 does place a responsibility on the headteacher for discipline and behaviour in school. The Department for Education issued guidelines recommending that schools should have an anti-bullying policy. According to the guidance:

> School staff must act – and importantly be seen to act – firmly against bullying whenever and wherever it appears. School behaviour policies ... should make specific reference to bullying. Governing bodies should regularly review their school's policy on bullying.
>
> School prospectuses and other documents issued to parents and pupils should make it clear that bullying will not be tolerated.

Clearly the Department for Education means for schools to take the problem of bullying seriously. But, as the Children's Legal Centre points out, the guidance does not create legal obligations on the part of the school. 'A school is not required by law to have an anti-bullying policy, but the guidance strongly recommends that it should as a matter of good practice.' This means that you, as a parent, can point out what the guidance says, but you cannot take the school to court for not having anti-bullying policies.

The very helpful Advisory Centre for Education (see Help Organisations) provides information and publications for parents about their children's education. The following is a brief description of the law as it applies to discipline in schools:

Education law makes no specific reference to bullying, but there are some aspects which could be considered relevant to bullying:

Discipline

Section 154 of the Education Act 1996 requires that:

'the articles of government for every county, voluntary and maintained special school shall provide for the conduct of the school to be under the direction of the governing body.'

Section 154 also provides:

'for it to be the duty of the headteacher to determine measures (which may include the making of rules and provision for enforcing them) to be taken with a view to –

i) promoting, among pupils, self-discipline and proper regard for authority

ii) encouraging good behaviour and respect for others on the part of pupils

iii) securing that the standard of behaviour of pupils is acceptable, and

iv) otherwise regulating the conduct of pupils.

In theory at least, this means that if parents thought that bullying were occurring in a school because of the failure of the headteacher or governors to fulfil properly their duties regarding behaviour and conduct they could complain to the Secretary of State under Section 497 of the Education Act 1996 that the headteacher/governors were in default of a statutory duty.

In Loco Parentis

The term 'in loco parentis' is used to describe the responsibility of a teacher towards the pupil and literally means 'in place of parent'. The teacher, therefore, assumes the responsibilities and obligations of a parent while the child is at school or otherwise under their charge (e.g. school trips, etc.).

Duty of Care

There is no dispute in law that the concept of duty of care applies to the role and circumstances of teachers in school.

The standard of care expected is that of any careful teacher and in the case of persons performing professional duties (such as teachers) would be the average amount of competence associated with the discharge of their professional duties.

Clearly one important difference between home and school will be that the teacher has to care for more children than a parent would at home and not every aspect of school life can be supervised. Consequently the 'prudent parent' role of the teacher cannot be identical to that of an actual parent.

JUDICIAL REVIEW

In the chapter on Working with the School, the procedure for complaining about bullying and inaction was set out. If you have exhausted all your appeals against the school or the Local Education Authority, you may seek a judicial review of their inaction. This must be done quickly and it is best to consult either the Children's Legal Centre or a solicitor for advice on the proper procedure. The point of a judicial review is to force the school or Local Education Authority to act to stop the bullying.

SUING THE SCHOOL FOR NEGLIGENCE

It is possible, but difficult, to sue the school or the Local Education Authority for damages to your child as a result of the school negligently failing to protect your child from bullying. There are several things that need to be proven in court including that your child has been bullied, that the school owed a duty of care to your child, that your child was harmed and that the harm was a direct result of the school failing to act to protect your child. Again, you need to ring the Children's Legal Centre for further information.

BULLYING IN THE COMMUNITY

One of the most difficult aspects of bullying to contend with is bullying in the community, away from the school. If the bullying is a spill-over from school bullying, then the school should work with you to try to stop it. If the bullying is completely unrelated to the school, then there are some steps parents can take. The real problem here is that often the parents of the bullies refuse to intervene to stop the bullying. Even worse, they are sometimes involved in the bullying themselves.

KIDSCAPE suggests that you:

1. keep a written record of all the incidents including dates, times, places and witnesses.

2. find out if the bullies go to a school which you can then contact to discuss ways to stop the bullying.

3. try, if possible, to have a quiet word with the bully's parents. This will obviously depend upon the age of the bully and the kind of family he or she comes from.

4. contact the Council Tenants' or Residents' Association for support. Also, if you have a Neighbourhood Watch scheme enlist their help to at least observe the bully's behaviour and to report it, if appropriate, to the police.

5. contact the Council Environmental Officer.

6. seek legal advice from the Home Organisations listed at the back of this book or consult a solicitor.

7. talk to local youth leader who may be able to quietly work with the children involved.

8. talk to local religious leader with community influence.

9. report what is happening to the police. Talk to the Community Liaison Officer and ask for their help. The response of police seems to vary greatly – some forces and officers are extremely helpful and others don't want to know. If the first person you speak to is unhelpful, ask to talk to the Officer in Charge or even try a different shift.

10. if possible, video or photograph the bullying. In fact, sometimes this acts as a deterrent to the bullies. No one wants proof on camera that they have been caught in the act.

11. take photographs of all injuries and keep a record of all medical treatment.

12. ask witnesses if they are prepared to back you up.

Sometimes straightforward solutions don't work. One mother rang KIDSCAPE to say that she had signed her son up for karate courses after months of bullying. After several lessons, the class staged a karate demonstration in front of their house. The bullying stopped overnight!

UNDERSTANDABLE CAUTION

In spite of some success stories when dealing with community bullying, I must sound a note of caution.

Although KIDSCAPE does recommend reporting bullying and other related crimes to the police, it is sometimes understandably difficult for parents to decide what they should do. This is especially hard when their child is frightened of retaliation if they do report the incident. Unfortunately, there have been some horrific cases in the news such as the family which endured bullying in their neighbourhood by local thugs over a period of twelve years. They were brave enough to sign petitions and report what happened, but it all ended tragically when their nineteen-year-old son was kicked to death by these same bullies while trying to defend his father. The fact that the bullies were tried and sentenced was no comfort.

Fortunately very few cases end as tragically as this, but bullying in the community when no effective action is taken, is one of the most difficult things to deal with. Several parents have told KIDSCAPE that they either voluntarily moved home to get away from bullies or begged the council to rehouse them if they were council tenants. It is a sad indictment that bullies can get away with making innocent people leave their homes, but that has happened.

LAST RESORT

If at all possible, the best way to sort out bullying problems is to nip them in the bud before they get out of hand. But should you find that your child is being bullied and you have tried all the suggestions in this book, your only option may be the law. I think the law should be strengthened to protect children and others from bullying. It is ridiculous that the thugs can prevail. It seems that, too often, might does make right.

POINTS TO REMEMBER

1. Bullying is not a criminal offence.

2. Schools are charged with a duty of care towards your child. If your child's education is being disrupted by bullying, you have a right to say to the school that you believe that the school is failing in its 'duty of care'.

3. Schools are not required by law to have a written disciplinary policy regarding bullying.

4. The Department for Education does issue guidance to schools recommending that they should have an anti-bullying policy. This is not, however, a legal requirement.

5. Some forms of bullying may amount to criminal behaviour – this includes a child being physically assaulted.

6. If your child has been left bruised, cut or bleeding by bullies, this may be classed as Actual Bodily Harm under Criminal Law.

7. If your child has had broken bones, severe bruising or been hospitalised as a result of bullying, this may be classed as Grievous Bodily Harm.

8. If your child is physically assaulted, get medical help and keep records and photographs as evidence.

9. Sometimes the threat of legal action galvanises schools to finally take firm steps to stop the bullying.

10. Seek advice from the Help Organisations listed at the back of this book or contact a solicitor if you would like to take legal action over a case of bullying.

11

HOME EDUCATION

Nine-year-old Kevin had been bullied for the past two years. Although his parents had worked with the school, the situation seemed to be out of control. The children waited for him to leave school some days and followed him home, knocking him off his bike, scattering his books and running away laughing. Kevin never knew when they would strike next. Sometimes they ambushed him in the toilets, sometimes on the way to school, sometimes on Saturday mornings outside his house. Kevin's life was one long series of horrible events, but no one seemed to be able to do anything effective.

Kevin's parents were told that maybe Kevin had a problem and that the bullying might be his own fault, although it was conceded that the chief bully had 'terrible problems at home'. The staff at the school were reluctant to call the bully's mother because she was abusive to them and blamed the school for everything. In this case the staff seemed to feel that getting rid of Kevin would solve some problems. Kevin was taken to see the educational psychologist who concluded that Kevin was 'nervous, withdrawn and unhappy'. The psychologist recommended that Kevin be sent to a special school.

This whole case made me furious. Here was a child who had been put through what I can only describe as torture over a two-year period. None of the adults involved, including his parents, was taking effective action to help him and stop the bullying. The staff had low morale and were overworked and stressed. There was no clear policy about bullying or discipline. Not surprisingly, there was also a fairly high staff turnover. Basically everyone was just keeping his or her head down and trying to get through the day. The children in the school were more or less in charge and bullying was rife.

Kevin's parents did their best, but they did not help Kevin because they decided to make the bullying an issue to get rid of the headteacher. Parents and staff lined up on one side or the other and there was an impasse. The Board of Governors was divided, as well, but continued to back the ineffective headteacher. Kevin's parents, instead of taking Kevin away from the school, felt honour bound to change the school so that Kevin and other children were not victimised. 'It is unfair that the staff and governors are not handling this so that Kevin can have an education free of harassment.'

I agree that they were right but, in the circumstances, they were completely unrealistic. In my opinion nothing was going to change in that school until there was a crisis in which someone really got hurt and the media found out. The best solution for Kevin was to get him out of that awful environment immediately. Only then could we know how badly he was damaged by all this.

After hearing about all that had taken place, we decided that the first step was to get a sick note from the doctor. Kevin was stressed to the point of wetting his bed, having nightmares, shaking and being completely unable to concentrate. I wondered what any adult, put through the kind of daily intimidation facing Kevin, would have done. Most probably quit his or her job.

When the school was told that Kevin was staying home, they told the parents that they were breaking the law by not sending their child to school and that they would be prosecuted. Many parents who ring the KIDSCAPE bully helpline say they have been told the same. This is shocking, since it is completely untrue. You do not have to send your child to school. Under Section 7 of the Education Act 1996, parents have a duty to see that their child receives 'Efficient full-time education suitable to his age, ability and aptitude, and to any special educational needs he may have, either by regular attendance at school or otherwise'. This means that you can educate your child at home if necessary.

Of course, most of us feel that school is the best place for children to be educated and we want them to be educated with other children of their own age and ability. But some children need either a short time away from school or are better off being educated at home for a variety of reasons.

So Kevin's parents kept him at home with the note from the GP going to the school stating that Kevin was under so much stress from bullying that it would be detrimental to his health for him to return. This brought Kevin and his parents some much-needed breathing space. The nightmares and bed wetting stopped overnight, just as it did when weekends and holidays saved Kevin from the bullies.

We then assessed Kevin and found that he was nervous and lacking in confidence but that this was because of the bullying. Kevin did not have any inherent problems that required special schooling. If anything, Kevin was a very bright little boy who had the ability to do any of the school work expected of a child his age. He had not been doing it because he could not think of anything except where the bullies were going to strike next.

The next step for Kevin was trying to find another school. This was difficult because there was only one primary school close by and that was the one that he was attending. The local authority refused to pay for Kevin's transportation to another school unless it was a special school because of the educational psychologist's assessment saying that Kevin should attend such a school. Kevin's parents did not have the means of getting him to another school.

Another factor to consider was that Kevin did not want to attend any school. He was adamant that he would kill himself if he were made to go to school. After much discussion, his parents and he agreed to trying Home Education until the end of the school year and then to decide what to do for the following year. When this decision was made, Kevin became a different child. His 'old' personality returned. He was more confident, humorous, cheeky and not at all withdrawn. It was hard to equate this new Kevin with the gibbering wreck of just a few weeks ago.

HOW TO DO IT

For Kevin school had become associated with such pain, humiliation and fear that, for the moment at least, there was no going back. What parents may not realise is that in addition to not having to send your child to school, there should be help from the Local Authority in educating your child at home though this does not always work out in practice!

As well as the Section 7 provision of the 1996 Education Act mentioned above, Section 9 of the same act states: '. . . the Local Authorities shall have regard to the general principle that, as far as it is compatible with the provision of suitable public expenditure, *pupils are to be educated in accordance with the wishes of their parents.*' (My italics.)

Note that both Northern Ireland and Scotland have the same or very similar provisions regarding home education and parents' wishes.

Fortunately, help is at hand for parents to negotiate the maze of Local Education Authorities and to successfully educate their children at home. If you are thinking of doing this, contact the extremely helpful organisations Home Education Advisory Service, Education Otherwise, and the Home Service (see Help Organisations) which will send you information. Some of these organisations also have helplines so you can talk to other parents who have gone this route.

For parents of teenagers who may need to study for GCSEs or A levels, correspondence colleges offer an alternative route. The Association of British Correspondence Colleges will put you in touch with reputable colleges. Some young people, badly bullied at school, come back two or three years later to sit their GCSEs or A levels. It is a shame that they have been put off their education by the bullies, but more power to them for bouncing back and being determined to get on with their lives.

Mercers College specialises in children's education from nursery age upwards. They provide courses for children who can't or don't want to attend school for any reason. Interestingly, they have seen a gradual increase in the numbers of children citing bullying as a reason for not going to school, a trend that KIDSCAPE has seen as well. The children work at home through correspondence courses and are sent work on a termly basis. This helps the children and their parents develop a regular schedule of work. Mercers College also have a team of tutors to whom the children are encouraged to send work regularly.

WHO PAYS?

The cost of courses at Mercers College and the correspondence colleges is usually met by the parents themselves, though in some cases funding has been available from a variety of sources including the Local Education Authority.

In general, the cost of home education does not have to be great, according to parents involved in it. Some parents manage even on income support, though they say it is not easy. It is an indication of the desperation that families come to that parents are willing to make whatever sacrifices it takes to get their children a decent education. It is a failing of the system that they should have to do this.

YOU DON'T HAVE TO BE A TEACHER

The comforting fact is that, because of the help available, you don't have to be a teacher or experienced in the education system to embark on home education. You don't even have to have formal qualifications. The Local Education Authority will arrange for an inspector to monitor your child's progress.

WAYS OF SOCIALISING

As for being with other children, some of the organisations mentioned above arrange for children to get together for social events and activities so that they don't miss out too much on that aspect of schooling. For a child who has been bullied out of school, this may not be important at first. Sometimes those children want nothing to do with other children. After the child has regained some self-esteem and confidence, however, making contact with other children can be very important.

WHAT'S THE PROCEDURE?

If you decide to remove your child from school to educate him or her at home, contact the Local Education Authority and ask that your child's name be removed from the school roll. You must inform both the school and the Local Education Authority or you may be cited for non-attendance of your child at school under the Education Act 1996, Section 444 for failure to de-register. You cannot just decide to take your child out without notification.

Write to the school and the Local Education Authority stating:

- the name of your child
- the date from which you are withdrawing your child
- the name of the school you are withdrawing your child from
- your intention and right under Section 7 Education Act 1996 to educate your child at home
- your desire that they ensure that your child is no longer registered at the school

It might be a good idea to send both these letters via registered post and to ask for a reply within a certain amount of time confirming what you have stated.

LOCAL EDUCATION AUTHORITY DUTY

You will find that some Local Education Authorities are very co-operative and will do everything they can to ensure that the transition from school to home education goes as smoothly as possible for your child. There are times, however, when difficulties with the Authority may arise.

One mother said to me that the Local Education Authority official said to her that if she withdrew her child from their system where they spend money on him, 'don't expect us to help you out. You're on your own.'

Under the Education Act 1996, Local Education Authorities have a duty to provide for children who cannot attend school because of exclusion or illness or other reasons. If a child does not attend school because he or she is in danger because of bullying, the child may be entitled to home tuition. Most parents say that the Local Education Authority insists upon a psychological assessment in these cases and the assessment often seems to blame their child for the bullying, as in the case of Kevin. This makes parents extremely angry and many just opt to pay for the education themselves.

PART-TIME SCHOOL

Some of the parents who have contacted KIDSCAPE have managed to work out a part-time school, part-time home-based education programme for their children. This helps children to build up their confidence while having a break from the tension, as well. Some children attend school for part of a day or one or two full days and study at home the rest of the time. There is no legal requirement for the school to do this and you cannot insist that they do. However, if you have a good relationship with the headteacher, this is one option for your child. Perhaps you would want to do this as a way of easing your child back into school after a period of home education.

Drawbacks

If you educate your child at home, you are opting out of the state education system, even if temporarily. Realistically you can expect no ongoing assistance from the Local Education Authority so it is a big step. It may be difficult for you if you are the sole parent in your family and have a job or if you are a couple and are both working outside the home just to make ends meet. It is not an easy option because it involves work and supervision from you. Also some parents make bad teachers for their own children – they are better off just being parents.

Pluses

For children like Kevin, education at home was a life-saver. His parents said that they thought he would have been either in a hospital with a nervous breakdown or dead without the option of home education. Kevin's parents found that they could act as his teachers (though Kevin said his father was better at it than his mother) and Kevin is now well on his way to feeling successful and self-confident for the first time in two years.

Another plus for home education is that education is not necessarily tied to the clock. If your child is doing something interesting he or she may continue past 3.45 or even start earlier in the morning, if you are alert early in the morning. In our house, mornings would be a problem for one of my children. In fact dragging him out of bed is a daily trial. One joy of home education for us, if we had done it, would have been not having to start at 8.30 a.m.!

POINTS TO REMEMBER

Home education is not the answer for every bullied child, but it is an option you may wish to consider if your child has become so disenchanted with school that he or she cannot cope any more.

1. According to the Education Act 1996, you do not have to send your child to school. You can educate your children at home.

2. According to the Education Act 1996, your wishes for your child's education must be considered.

3. There are several organisations which can help you set up home education.

4. There are correspondence colleges which will arrange for your child to have a course of work or to study for GCSEs or A levels.

5. You don't have to be a teacher to educate your child at home.

6. Parents usually bear the entire cost of home education.

7. If your child is educated at home, he or she can meet with other children for social events or activities through some of the home education organisations.

8. It may be possible to arrange for your child to attend school part-time and work at home part-time. There is no obligation on the part of the school to do this.

9. Educating your child at home places an extra burden on you and the entire family. Make sure you find out as much as possible when making your decision.

10. Home education has been the salvation of many bullied children. It can bring you and your child closer together and help your child to build up his or her self-esteem and confidence.

HELP ORGANISATIONS

BOOKS

Mail Order Booksellers with up-to-date catalogues on bullying and disruptive behaviour:

Abbey Books
4 Bank View Road
Derby
DE3 1EL
Tel: 01332 290021

Forum Bookshop
86 Abbey Street
Derby
DE22 3SQ
Tel: 01332 368039

ANOREXIA/BULIMIA/OTHER EATING DISORDERS

The following organisations will give advice and/or therapy for those suffering from eating disorders (and their families):

Eating Disorders Association (EDA)
Sackville Place
44/48 Magdalen Street
Norwich NR3 1JU
Tel: 01603 621414

The National Centre for Eating Disorders
11 Esher Place Avenue
Esher
Surrey KT10 8PU
Tel: 01372 469493

BEREAVEMENT

The Compassionate Friends
53 North Street
Bristol BS3 1EN
Tel: 01179 665202

Helpline: 0117 9539639   9.30 a.m. to 5 p.m. Mon to Fri

A nationwide (and international) self-help organisation of parents whose child of any age, including adult, has died through accident, illness, murder or suicide. A postal library and leaflets are also available.

Cruse
126 Sheen Road
Richmond
Surrey TW9 1UR
Tel: 0181 332 7227   9.30 a.m. to 5 p.m. Mon to Fri

Offers counselling for all bereavements.

COUNSELLING, ADVICE AND INFORMATION

Anti-Bullying Campaign
Tel: 0171 378 1446

Helpline for bullied children and parents.

British Association of Counselling (BAC)
1 Regent Place
Rugby
Warwickshire CV21 2VT

Refers people to qualified counsellors. Send A5 size SAE for list of counsellors in your local area.

ChildLine
Tel: 0800 1111

24-hour freephone helpline for children and young people.

Family Service Units
207 Old Marylebone Road
London NW1 5QP
Tel: 0171 402 5175

Provides family counselling in branches throughout England.
Ring to obtain number of your local branch.

KIDSCAPE
152 Buckingham Palace Road
London SW1W 9TR
Tel: 0171 730 3300   10 a.m. to 4 p.m. Mon to Fri

Helpline for parents of bullied or bullying children. Send a
large SAE for copies of three free booklets about bullying and
information about training courses.

National Society for the Prevention of Cruelty to Children
Tel: 0800 800 500

24-hour free helpline for anyone concerned about child abuse
or bullying.

Samaritans
Tel: 0345 909090

24-hour helpline for anyone with problems. Some areas have
drop-in centres.

Victim Support Scheme
National Office
Cranmer House
39 Brixton Road
London SW9 6DZ
Tel: Local directory or ring 0171 735 9166 for information
about local numbers.

A nationwide network of support groups offering practical help and advice to victims of bullying, violence and crime.

Youth Access
1A Taylor's Yard
67 Alderbrook Road
London SW12 8AD
Tel: 0181 772 9900

Provides names and addresses of local free counselling services to young people. Telephone, or write enclosing an SAE.

DIVORCE/SEPARATION

National Family Mediation
9 Tavistock Place
London WC1H 9SN
Tel: 0171 383 5993

Helps couples (married or unmarried) going through a separation or divorce to make joint decisions about a range of issues, with particular focus on arrangements for their children. For information ring or send a large SAE for leaflets.

National Step-Family Association
18 Hatton Place
London EC1N 8RU
Tel: 0990 168 388   2 p.m. to 5 p.m. and 7 p.m. to 10 p.m. Mon to Fri

Offers support to all members of step-families and those who work with them. Send a large SAE for information pack.

Relate Marriage Guidance
Little Church Street
Rugby CV21 3AP
Tel: 01788 573241

Provides advice for couples (married or unmarried) who are experiencing relationship problems. For the telephone number of the Relate office near you, check your local directory under RELATE or ring the national headquarters for a referral. Send a large self-addressed envelope for leaflets.

FAMILIES

Exploring Parenthood (EP)
4 Ivory Place
Treadgold Street
London W11 4BP
Tel: 0171 221 6681 10 a.m. to 4 p.m. Mon to Fri

Provides professional support and advice to all parents who experience problems from time to time. Easy access to professional advice and support.

Gingerbread
16–17 Clerkenwell Close
London EC1R OAA
Tel: 0171 336 8184

Offers support, information and social activities for one-parent families.

National Council for One-Parent Families
255 Kentish Town Road
London NW5 2LX
Tel: 0171 267 1361

Write or telephone for practical literature regarding issues such as housing, separation, getting back to work, etc. or for a referral to a local help agency.

Parents Anonymous
6 Manor Gardens
London N7 6LA
Tel: 0171 263 8918. Answerphone – gives telephone numbers of volunteers who are on duty. They aim to give a 24-hour service.

Parents Anonymous offers a listening service plus help and support to parents who are experiencing problems with any issues regarding children and young people.

Parent-Line
Endway House
The Endway
Benfleet
Essex SS7 2AN
Tel: 01702 559900   9 a.m. to 6 p.m. Mon to Fri, 1 p.m to 6 p.m. Sat. After hours number supplied on answerphone.

Provides support for parents under stress, therefore maximising a family's capacity for its children.

Parent Network
44–46 Caversham Road
London NW5 2DS
Tel: 0171 485 8535

Programmes to equip parents to feel supported and encouraged whilst doing the most important job of raising children.

HOME EDUCATION

Education Otherwise
Tel: 0891 518303. Answerphone with a list of regional contact numbers

Home Education Advisory Service
PO Box 98, Welwyn Garden City, Herts. AL8 6AN

Provides support for children to help them get back into the local education system. Send large SAE for comprehensive information pack.

The Home Service
48 Heton Moor Road
Heton Moor
Stockport SK4 4NX
Tel: 01246 410122

Provides support for Christian families wishing to educate children at home.

Mercers College
Tel: 01920 465926

Provides correspondence courses for children from nursery school age upwards.

Association of British Correspondence Colleges
Tel: 0181 544 9559

Provides correspondence courses for young people wishing to do GCSEs and A levels.

LEARNING DIFFICULTIES

Dyslexic Institute
152 Buckingham Palace Road
London SW1W 9TR
Tel: 0171 730 8890

Carries out assessments of children in centres throughout the country and operates a national teaching network. For further information and/or copies of their leaflets, ring or send an SAE.

LEGAL ADVICE

Advisory Centre for Education (ACE)
1B Aberdeen Studios
22 Highbury Grove
London N5 2EA
Helpline Tel: 0171 354 8321   2 to 5 p.m. Mon to Fri

Gives free advice for parents and publications for parents and professionals about education law.

Children's Legal Centre
Tel: 01206 873820   2 to 5 p.m. Mon to Fri

Provides free legal advice regarding children and the law. They have available a comprehensive leaflet regarding bullying and the law.

Education Law Association (ELAS)
29 South Drive
Ferring
Worthing
West Sussex BN12 5QU
Tel: 01903 504 949

Gives names and addresses of solicitors throughout the country who deal with education law.

Scottish Child Law Centre
Lion Chambers
170 Hope Street
Glasgow G2 2TU
Tel: 0141 226 3737 10 a.m. to 4 p.m. Tues to Fri

Provides free legal advice about children and Scottish law.

PLAYGROUND DESIGN

Learning through Landscapes
Third Floor, Southside Offices
The Law Courts
Winchester
Hants
Tel: 01962 846258

Information, books and videos on improving playgrounds. It may be useful to put schools in contact with them.

PUNISHMENT

End Physical Punishment of Children (EPOCH)
77 Holloway Road
London N7 8JZ
Tel: 0171 700 0627

National campaign to end all physical punishment of children. It provides leaflets and posters. Send a large SAE for a free copy of their No Smacking leaflet.

SCHOOL PHOBIA

No Panic
93 Brands Farm Way
Randlay
Telford
Shropshire TF3 2JQ
Helpline Tel: 01952 590545   10 a.m. to 4 p.m. Mon to Fri

Information and advice for all types of phobia.

SELF-DEFENCE

Quindo
The Quindo Centre
2 West Heath Drive
London NW11 7QH
Tel: 0181 455 8698

Help Organisations

Ki Federation of Great Britain
Tel: 01278 781166

Will put you in contact with local organisations.

Also contact local authorities for classes in martial arts.

RESOURCES (BOOKS, LEAFLETS)

FREE LEAFLETS FOR PARENTS AND CHILDREN

PREVENTING BULLYING: A Parent's Guide
20-page booklet with practical advice for parents.

STOP BULLYING!
20-page booklet with suggestions for parents, teacher and children.

YOU CAN BEAT BULLYING!
20-page booklet for young people.

Send a large self-addressed stamped envelope to KIDSCAPE, 152 Buckingham Palace Road, London SW1W 9TR for a free copy of any of the leaflets.

BOOKS FOR PARENTS

501 WAYS TO BE A GOOD PARENT
Author: Michele Elliott
Publisher: Hodder & Stoughton
ISBN   0-340-64903-8

BAD BEHAVIOUR
Author: John Pearce
Publisher: Thorsons
ISBN   0-7225-1723-8

THE BULLYING PROBLEM: How to Deal with Difficult Children
Author: Alan Train
Publisher: A Condor Book, Souvenir Press (E&A Ltd)
ISBN   0-285-63255-8

CONFIDENT CHILDREN: A Parents' Guide to Helping Children Feel Good
Author: Gael Lindenfield
Publisher: Thorsons
ISBN   0-7225-2824-8

FIGHTING, TEASING AND BULLYING
Author: John Pearce
Publisher: Thorsons
ISBN   0-7225-1722-X

HELPING CHILDREN COPE WITH BULLYING
Author: Sarah Lawson

Publisher: Sheldon Press
ISBN   0-85969-683-9

HELPING CHILDREN COPE WITH STRESS
Author: Ursula Markham
Publisher: Sheldon Press
ISBN   0-85969-608-1

HOW TO STAND UP FOR YOURSELF
Author: Paul Hauck
Publisher: Sheldon Press
ISBN   0-85969-335-X

OVERCOMING YOUR NERVES
Author: Tony Lake
Publisher: Sheldon Press
ISBN   0-85969-590-5

TANTRUMS AND TEMPERS
Author: John Pearce
Publisher: Thorsons
ISBN   0-7225-1721-1

BOOKS FOR PROFESSIONALS

ASSERTION TRAINING: How to be who you really are
Author: S. Rees & R. Graham
Publisher: Routledge
ISBN   0-415-01073-X

BULLIES AND VICTIMS IN SCHOOLS
Author: Valerie Besag
Publisher: Open University Press
ISBN   0-335-0954222-9

BULLYING: An Annotated Bibliography of Literature and Resources
Author: Alison Skinner
Publisher: Youth Work Press
ISBN   0-86155-143-5

BULLYING: A COMMUNITY APPROACH
Author: Brendan Byrne
Publisher: The Columbia Press
ISBN   1-85607-103-0

BULLYING: A PRACTICAL GUIDE TO COPING FOR SCHOOLS
Author: Edited by Michele Elliott
Publisher: Pitman (also available from KIDSCAPE)

THE BULLYING PROBLEM
Author: Alan Train
Publisher: Souvenir Press
ISBN 0-285-63255-8

BULLYING AT SCHOOL: What we know and what we can do
Author: Dan Olweus
Publisher: Blackwell
ISBN   0-273-626922

COPING WITH BULLYING IN SCHOOLS
Author: Brendan Byrne
Publisher: Cassell
ISBN   0-304-33071-X

HOW TO STOP BULLYING:
A KIDSCAPE Training Guide
Author: Michele Elliott & Jane Kilpatrick
Publisher: KIDSCAPE
ISBN   1-872572-01-4

A POSITIVE APPROACH TO BULLYING
Author: Eve Brock
Publisher: Longman
ISBN   0-582-21490-4

POSITIVE SCHOOL DISCIPLINE
Author: Margaret Cowin, Liz Freeman, et al.
Publisher: Longman
ISBN   0-582-08713-9

PRACTICAL APPROACHES TO BULLYING
Author: Peter K. Smith & David Thompson
Publisher: David Fulton Publishers
ISBN   1-85346-159-8

SCHOOL BULLYING
Author: Peter K. Smith & Sonia Sharp
Publisher: Routledge
ISBN   0-415-10373-8

SOME APPROACHES TO BULLYING
Author: Des Mason
Available from Governors Support Unit, South Glamorgan
Council

TEENSCAPE
Author: Michele Elliott
Publisher: Health Education Authority (also available from
KIDSCAPE)
ISBN   1-85448-069-3

TURN YOUR SCHOOL ROUND
Author: Jenny Mosley
Publisher: LDA
ISBN   1-85503-174-4

'YOU KNOW THE FAIR RULE'
Author: Bill Rogers
Publisher: Longman
ISBN   0-582-08672-8

YOUNG FRIENDS
Author: Sue Roffey, Tony Tarrant, Karen Majors
Publisher: Cassell
ISBN   0-304-32989-4

WE CAN STOP IT
Author: Hilary Claire
Publisher: Islington Safer Cities Project

Reducing bullying in the playground

'CAN I STAY IN TODAY MISS?'
Author: Carol Ross and Amanda Ryan
Publisher: Trentham Books
ISBN   0-948080-42-6

CHILDREN'S GAMES IN STREET AND PLAYGROUND
Author: Iona & Peter Opie
Publisher: Oxford University Press
ISBN   0-19-281489-3

THE OUTDOOR CLASSROOM
Author: Edited by Brian Keaney & Bill Lucas
Publisher: Scholastic
ISBN   0-590-53034-8

PLAYTIME IN THE PRIMARY SCHOOL
Author: Peter Blatchford
Publisher: Routledge
ISBN   0-415-09861-0

USING SCHOOL GROUNDS AS AN EDUCATIONAL RESOURCE
Author: Kirsty Young
Available from Learning Through Landscapes, Tel. 01962 846258
ISBN   1-872865-04-6

VIDEOS

BULLYING: FACE IT, STOP IT, HOW
20 mins with accompanying notes (32 pages)
Produced by Cumbria Education Service with the Alfred Barrow School, Barrow-in-Furness, Cumbria. Tel. 01229 827 355.

KICKS AND INSULTS
20 mins
Produced by Educational Media Film & Video Ltd, Harrow, Middx. Tel. 0181 868 1908/1915

ONLY PLAYING MISS
56 mins (Playscript also available)
Produced by Neti-Neti Theatre Company, London, Tel. 0171 272 7302

STAMP OUT BULLYING
With accompanying book
Produced by Lame Duck Publishing
ISBN   1-873942-10-9

STICKS AND STONES
20 mins for 12 to 16-year-olds
Produced by Central Television in association with KIDSCAPE
Available from KIDSCAPE, Tel. 0171 730 3300

BOOKS FOR CHILDREN

Books for younger children:

THE ANTI COLOURING BOOK
Author: Susan Striker/Edward Kimmell
Publisher: Hippo
ISBN   0-590-70011-1   Age 4+

THE BAD TEMPERED LADYBIRD
Author: Eric Carle
Publisher: Picture Puffin
ISBN   0-14-050398-6   Age 3+

BEING BULLIED
Author: Kate Petty and Charlotte Firmin
Publisher: Bracken Books
ISBN   1-85170-955-X   Age 5–8

BILL'S NEW FROCK
Author: Anne Fine
Publisher: Mammoth
ISBN   0-7497-0305-9   Age 7–9

BOY ON A BUS
Author: Dermot McKay
Publisher: Grosvenor Books
ISBN   1-85239-009-3   Age 7–11

BULLIES AND GANGS
Author: Julie Johnson
Publisher: Watts Books   Age 5–9
ISBN   0-7496-2558-9

THE BULLIES MEET THE WILLOW ST KIDS
Author: Michele Elliott
Publisher: Piccolo (also available from KIDSCAPE, £3.50)
ISBN   0-330-32800-X   Age 7–11

BULLY
Author: David Hughes
Publisher: Walker Books
ISBN   0-7445-2169-6   Age 3–6

BULLY FOR YOU
Publisher: Child's Play
ISBN   0-85953-365-4   Age 4–7

FEELING HAPPY FEELING SAFE
Author: Michele Elliott
Publisher: Hodder & Stoughton (also available from
KIDSCAPE)
ISBN   0-340-55386-3   Age 2–6

FEELING LEFT OUT
Author: Kate Petty and Charlotte Firmin
Publisher: Bracken House
ISBN   1-85170-954-1   Age 5–8

I WON'T GO THERE AGAIN
Author: Susan Hill
Publisher: Walker Books
ISBN   0-7445-2091-6   Age 3 +

MAKING FRIENDS
Author: Kate Petty and Charlotte Firmin
Publisher: Bracken Books
ISBN   1-85170-956-8   Age 5–8

PLAYING THE GAME
Author: Kate Petty and Charlotte Firmin
Publisher: Bracken Books
ISBN   1-85170-953-3   Age 5–8

RHYME STEW
Author: Roald Dahl
Publisher: Jonathan Cape
ISBN   0-224-02660-7   Age 6+

ROSIE AND THE PAVEMENT BEARS
Author: Susie Jenkin-Pearce
Publisher: Red Fox
ISBN   0-09-972090-6   Age 4+

THE TWITS
Author: Roald Dahl
Publisher: Puffin
ISBN   0-14-031406-7   Age 6+

THE TROUBLE WITH THE TUCKER TWINS
Author: Rose Impey & Maureen Galvani
Publisher: Picture Puffins
ISBN   0-14-054089-X   Age 4–6

Books for older children and teens:

THE BAILEY GAME
Author: Celia Rees
Publisher: Piper
ISBN   0-330-33326-7   Age 12–Teen

BULLIES
Author: Ed Wick
Publisher: Kingsway
ISBN   0-85476-406-2   Age 12–Teen

BULLY
Author: Yvonne Coppard
Publisher: Red Fox
ISBN   0-09-983860-5   Age 10–Teen

THE BULLYBUSTERS JOKE BOOK
Author: John Byrne
Publisher: Red Fox
ISBN   0-09-960981-9   Age 9–Teen

CHICKEN
Author: Alan Gibbons
Publisher: Orion Children's Books
ISBN   1-85881-051-5   Age 9–12

THE CHOCOLATE WAR
Author: Robert Cormier
Publisher: Lions, Tracks
ISBN   0-00671765-9   Age 9–13

DON'T PICK ON ME
Author: Rosemary Stones
Publisher: Piccadilly
ISBN   1-85881-053-1   Age 10–Teen

THE FISH FLY LOW
Author: Steve May
Publisher: Mammoth
ISBN   0-7497-1410-7   Age 10–Teen

LORD OF THE FLIES
Author: William Golding
Publisher: Faber and Faber
ISBN   0-5710-8483-4   Age 12–Teen

THE PRESENT TAKERS
Author: Aidern Chambers
Publisher: Mammoth
ISBN   0-7497-0700-3   Age 12–Teen

THE TRIAL OF ANNA COTMAN
Author: V. Alcock
Publisher: Mammoth/Octopus
ISBN   0-7497-0978-2   Age 10–Teen

WHOSE SIDE ARE YOU ON?
Author: Alan Gibbons
Publisher: Orion Children's Books
ISBN   1-85881-053-1   Age 9–12

INDEX

Index

Index

Index

Index

love and support, 40, 51, 97, 100, 150, 152
lunch-room staff, 107

making friends, 101–19, 158
  change behaviour, 115–16
  decide on a plan, 104–5
  develop new skills, activities,
    interests, 117
  find out what is happening, 103–4
  get help at school, 105, 107
  invite children over, 112–13
  it doesn't always work out, 116–17,
    119
  points to remember, 118–19
  roleplay, 111–12
  talk about friendship, 108–10
  watch what is happening, 113–14
medical evidence, 200, 209, 212
medical problems, 69, 148, 158, 216, 217
menacing, 3
Mercers College, 219, 220
middle schools, 12
money
  demanding, 3, 43
  extorting, 18
  money problems in the bully's family,
    59
  stolen by the bully, 5, 75
  stolen by the victim to pay the bully, 5
monitoring, 8, 107, 145, 220
moving home, 210–11
MPs (Members of Parliament), 128–9

name-calling, 3, 12, 13, 17, 19, 22, 36–7,
  43, 139, 154, 202
National Confederation of Parent
  Teacher Associations, 188, 198
Neighbourhood Watch, 209
nightmares, 4, 5, 216
Northern Ireland, 219
nursery schools see bullying the babies

Olweus, Dan, 3, 20, 58
ostracism, 1, 18, 22, 25, 27, 155

parents
  as bullies, 163, 181–2

'hysterical', 166, 187, 188, 197
  as teachers, 220, 223, 225, 226
  use of humour, 176, 183
  see also home education; taking care
    of yourself
parents' groups, 192
part-time school, 223, 227
peer pressure, 16, 63
perpetual victims, 10, 27–8, 144, 150,
  151, 153
personal habits, 34, 103, 115, 116
photographs of bullying/injuries, 209,
  212
physical bullying, 1, 3, 5, 8, 12, 13, 17, 19,
  22, 199
  and the law, 200, 212
  young children, 139, 140, 141
plan, making a
  behaviour plan, 149
  building self-esteem, 96–7
  making friends, 104–5
playground design, 239
playground supervisors, 70, 107
police, 52, 73, 129, 162, 199, 202, 203, 209
  KIDSCAPE recommendations on
    calling the police, 200, 210
positive thinking, 92, 94, 96
possessions
  arrange a place for, 174
  demanding, 3
  destruction/vandalising of, 1, 4, 202
  theft, 5, 17, 19, 75
power
  bullying to achieve, 9
  imbalance of, 23
  power struggles, 178–9
praise, 60, 66, 68, 73, 78–80, 97, 98, 150,
  167, 169, 183
press, the, 129
prison, bullies in, 20
professional help, seeking, 69, 150, 196
protection, 22, 30, 31–2, 51, 207, 208, 211
psychological assessment, 215, 218, 222
punishment, physical, 55, 179
  organisation, 239–40

questionnaire, anonymous, 8

261

Index

Index

Index